CHANGED

REAL LIVES IN A REAL WORLD

CARLOS CAMACHO AND MANNY CRUZ
COMPILERS

Pacific Press® Publishing Association
Nampa, Idaho
Oshawa, Ontario, Canada
www.pacificpress.com

**North American Division
Youth & Young Adult Ministries**
Silver Spring, Maryland
www.adventistyouthministries.org

Cover design by Josue Murillo
Inside design by Aaron Troia

Copyright © 2012 by Pacific Press® Publishing Association
Printed in the United States of America

The authors assume full responsibility for the accuracy of all facts and quotations as cited in this book.

Scripture quotations from *The Message.* Copyright © by Eugene H. Peterson, 1993, 1994, 1995. Used by permission of NavPress Publishing Group.

Scriptures quoted from the NIV are from THE HOLY BIBLE, NEW INTERNATIONAL VERSION®, NIV®. Copyright © 1973, 1978, 1984, 2011 by Biblica, Inc.™ Used by permission. All rights reserved worldwide.

Scriptures quoted from NKJV are from The New King James Version, copyright © 1979, 1980, 1982, Thomas Nelson, Inc., Publishers.

Scriptures quoted from the KJV are from the King James Version of the Bible.

Additional copies of this book are available by calling toll-free 1-800-765-6955 or by visiting http://www.adventistbookcenter.com.

ISBN 13: 978-0-8163-2688-4
ISBN 10: 0-8163-2688-6

12 13 14 15 16 • 5 4 3 2 1

CONTENTS

INTRODUCTION

CHANGED *3* IS THE *THIRD* CHANGED BOOK IN what has now become a series of awesome readings for youth and young adults. It is also part of the North American Division *Changed Latino Youth Evangelism initiative for 2012*. Chances are you will probably hear more about it through your pastor or friends maybe (or you can go to www.ChangedLatinoYouth .com). However, this book is a little different than the first two in that the stories deal with everyday life temptations, like sex, guilt, dating, family, loss, and decision making among other important issues. Each chapter has been written with you in mind.

As you read this book, you may identify with a story or two or you may know someone who will; you know how it is, many of us are going through "stuff" and that's just how life is. As a young person living in today's world, you face stuff, no doubt about that; sometimes you deal with stuff that not even your family or friends know about, and life just seems so hard. It is in those moments and through them that you can truly experience God.

The stories in this book will point that out. This book is not going to give you all the answers to all your questions, but it will give you hope and will remind you that there is a God, a loving God who desires to change you. Why? Because He loves you unconditionally; He is the One who truly understands you. He created you. He set out to save you. You are His child. You are precious to Him.

So read the book, share the book, talk about the book, but always remember that your life is being *changed* by the God who doesn't change but that *changes you*. Have you been *changed*?

Manny Cruz
Youth and young adults associate director
for the North American Division

IT ALL STARTS RIGHT HERE ESE

JOSÉ VICENTE ROJAS

LET ME JUST TELL YOU THIS AS YOU START READING this book: it all starts right here, *ese* (dude)! Then God changes you in ways you cannot imagine! God can and will mess with you in ways beyond your wildest dreams because you are His, and He loves you unconditionally! Now, hear me out.

A FRESHMAN IN HIGH SCHOOL

I met this dude in high school named Johnny Perez. Johnny was once a tough guy from Farmersville, a small agricultural town in the Central Valley of California. Although his town was very small, they still had a gang problem among their youth. Johnny had just graduated from a Christian high school, Monterey Bay Academy, with the class of 1975, and was working that summer to pay off his school bill.

I had deep respect for Johnny because he was known as "the Lizard," the gang nickname he had earned on the streets. This gave Johnny credentials in my book. He had earned his way to being a *veterano,* a title given to gang members who no longer have anything to prove, meaning that they are established.

What was most disarming to me about Johnny was his personality. He had become a gentle, loving guy who reached out to me with complete acceptance and a totally cool Chicano attitude, much like my brother Gerry (Li'l Bosco) had always done for me. I noticed that Johnny took a special interest in me, and he would dedicate some of his time to hang out; he always talked to me as if I were his little brother too. At the end of that summer, Johnny left and went home, while I stayed and started the new school year.

THE QUIET GUY

I turned sixteen years old in the spring of that school year and was well into my sophomore year. As a teenager I had heard that young people were getting worse and worse, and indeed there were many stories to justify that opinion in the media and in the community. But I was still one of those "neutral" students on campus and came to be labeled as "the quietest person" in the sophomore class. I was known as a shy kid, but not because it was true; I was simply intimidated by life and didn't know how I fit in.

IT STARTS HERE, *ESE*!

On a particularly warm Sunday morning after breakfast, as I was walking back to the dormitory where I lived, I had guitars on my mind, and I wanted to hurry and get to the room. Suddenly, I heard the sounds of thousands of birds. As I looked up into the sky, a beehivelike cloud of noisy migrating blackbirds moved across the campus. I stood for a moment deeply transfixed by the experience. Then I suddenly felt a tap on my shoulder. It was Johnny Perez.

Johnny had come to visit campus for the weekend and had come to look me up to hang out for a while. As we stood together watching the birds, he began to talk about his experience in Christ. Johnny was not sophisticated by traditional definitions, but his life spoke of the sophistication of the Holy Spirit deep in his soul. We talked all morning that day as Johnny testified to what God had done in his life since he had surrendered himself completely to Jesus.

Then the moment came when Johnny turned to me and said, "It starts here, *ese*." I listened silently as Johnny then invited me to join him in dedicating my life to Christ. I instinctively reminded him that I was already baptized, and Johnny agreed that my baptism had been an important step. He informed me that I could now move further in the commitment of my life to God.

Johnny added that if I were going to do true ministry and have something *real* to share, it all needed to start with this most basic of all commitments, a commitment of life itself to God, what inspired writers have referred to as "conversion." We inched back to the dorm and went to my room.

I will always treasure the memory of that day as we knelt in room 232 on the top south hall of the boys' dormitory. Johnny and I prayed a prayer, which, in its simplicity, brought out my deepest commitment for life. Jesus became my Lord and Savior that spring day in 1976.

A HIGHER CALLING

This testimony is mine; it's like many other stories that are told as evidence of God's power to change lives. But I am dumbfounded by what this experience in Christ did for me. Giving my life to Jesus is something that I had heard of for a long time. I had thought that commitment to Christ was merely a commitment of beliefs and behaviors. But I soon discovered that Jesus is the experience of a lifetime that impacts not only our lives but also the lives of others around us. From that day onward, I have learned that to live Jesus is to share Him like never before.

When you give your life to God, something powerful happens. You are hooking up with the God of the universe! The Lord will begin to use your life to bless others. It's not *what* you know that makes this incredible, it's *who* you know. The apostle wrote in the Bible, "Christ *in* me, the hope of glory!" He was telling the truth because your life becomes a message to others. God will take your talents and make them grow. You begin to serve your community as you serve God, and that's what happened to me.

MY FIRST SERMON

The very week after I gave my life to Christ, I was asked to join a student group that took programs to churches on behalf of the school. One day not long after that, as our group was visiting the Selma, California, Seventh-day Adventist Church, our program ended early. The pastor suddenly realized that he had almost half an hour of church service left! After an awkward silence, the pastor, scanning the front pew of nervous students, proceeded to invite *me* to get up and finish the program! He whispered into my ear, saying, "You guys ended a whole half hour early; you're going to have to get up and preach!"

I was stunned. My knees shook with an intense fear. I felt sick to my stomach. I hesitated for what seemed like seven seconds, a very long time when you're afraid! Then I got up to that pulpit and preached about the final scenes of the cross of Christ. The depictions of our Savior's suffering in that unprepared sermon visibly wrenched the congregation at times. People obviously felt uncomfortable almost literally watching Jesus die before them through my descriptive language. I had no way of professionally sanitizing into simple words the penalty Christ bore for our sins.

In hindsight, I now realize just how blunt and plain the sermon had been. From that day forward, however, I have continued to intentionally take people past the cross of Jesus in my sermons, no matter what the topic is. This occurred long before I knew that I would some-day study for the ministry. At the age of sixteen, I preached my first official sermon. I was sick with the nausea of stage fright for the rest of the day.

CALLED TO SERVE

Only two months later, as the summer approached, I was invited by a literature evangelist named David Lewis to participate in a program called "Community Crusade Against Drugs," in the city of San Francisco. Although I was only sixteen, my parents gave permission for me to join the team of students far from home. We worked directly on the streets of the city and went door to door, taking a message of drug-free living in the name of Jesus.

That summer was my first shot at bachelor life. My friends tell me I have never been the same since. I saw that there is a large world of people dying anonymously in their sins. But each of these people, living deep in the cities of the world, is a wonderful human being in need of someone to love them. Those inner-city people, who some irreverently refer to as the scum of the earth, are souls for whom Christ willingly gave up His life to save.

This experience profoundly impacted the intensity of my outlook on life and my zeal for the gospel ministry. My time working on Dave's team in San Francisco pushed me into a Christianity that constantly seeks to make things happen in the community. The Lord also taught me to be faithful in the simple tasks of serving others.

AWESOME DIVINE APPOINTMENTS

One morning the phone rang during breakfast at the Spanish church where I lived with my roommate. The call was from the University of California Medical Center down the peninsula on the other side of San Francisco. A nurse at the other end of the line said that a patient was going to have serious surgery. The patient was a Seventh-day Adventist and was not from the area. She was hoping that an Adventist pastor could visit her before surgery the next day.

I responded that our church's pastor spoke no English and that she would be better served if the pastor from the English-speaking church were to visit her. After giving the phone number of the San Francisco Tabernacle Church, my roommate and I finished breakfast and prepared for the day's activities on the streets of the city.

I hurriedly finished reading a favorite book that morning also. The book, titled *A Field Guide to Wilderness Living,* was an inspiring collection of tips for living in the harshest of wilderness conditions. I had loved this book so much that I had it hardbound after buying it. I took the book with me in the car as we drove to the section of San Francisco we were to work in that day.

That night after we dropped off the last student team member, my roommate and I went to a fast-food restaurant on the corner of Market and Seventh Streets. The time was about 11:30 P.M., and we sat quietly at the table.

Suddenly, it hit us both at the same moment: with a sense of certainty we exclaimed that no one had gone to see the woman at the hospital that day! Neither one of us could say how we knew this, but we did. We simply felt sure that the hospital probably did not reach anyone to go see the woman facing serious surgery the next morning.

We quickly picked up our food and ran out to the car. The drive across San Francisco is like no other trip in the world. When climbing the many hills that dominate the landscape, you often have to stop on inclines that feel more like a wall than a street. We finally reached the hospital and parked a block away, for even at that hour, parking was scarce.

The hospital is a huge structure with many departments and patient floors. Yet with confidence, we went directly to the ninth floor. When we emerged from the elevator, we saw a long, dark hallway. Perhaps a hundred feet down, a small light lit the hallway where the nurses' station was located. Two worried faces peered cautiously in our direction as we walked down the hallway. My roommate's rubber flip-flops slapped against the bottom of his feet, and our bell-bottom pants matched our shoulder-length hair, forming a silhouette that truly frightened the nurses at that hour of the night.

The nurses wanted to call security, but it was too late; by then we stood before them, smiling and asking for a favor. I stated that we were representing the Seventh-day Adventist Church and had come to visit a patient who was having surgery in a few hours. The nurse reminded us that visiting hours had ended more than four hours earlier. We insisted that our visit was pastoral and that we had to see the patient. One of the nurses finally said, "Well, I don't like this, but follow me, and I'll take you to her."

We walked down the hall to a room where the nurse opened the door and let us in. We were amazed to find that, indeed, no one had come to see the patient. As we walked into the room, the time was exactly midnight. A night light provided just enough light to see a woman sitting up in bed and in tears. The woman exclaimed, "Don't tell me you're Adventists!" We smiled and said that we were. She said, "I had all but given up, and the Lord knew what He was going to do. At the stroke of midnight He has sent me two hippie Adventists to minister to me!"

The moment was the kind I had read about in books, one of those miracle moments in the life of a Christian, as God meets someone's need through His people. We bonded almost immediately as the patient told us of her journey to that place. She stated that she now knew that she was ready for surgery since God had sent us to her.

After that, she led us in prayer and thanked God for the miracle of ministry. A miracle that shows God cares and that He will not forsake us. We had gone to minister to her, but instead she was ministering to us. I learned that summer the essence of ministry: *freely you give and freely you receive.*

After prayer the woman said, "My name is Catherine Gearing. Have you read my book, *A Field Guide to Wilderness Living*?" My jaw must have dropped to the floor! This was my favorite book! The book I had just finished reading that very day! We spent the next hour celebrating how God shows His love by bringing His people together. As we drove back across the peninsula that night, I held Catherine's book in my hands, knowing that we had done God's will in ministry that day. Catherine Gearing's surgery went very well the next day.

UNLEASHED TO SERVE OTHERS

When I returned to school at the end of that summer, I was a new person. What God did in me in San Francisco was release me from the limitations I myself had set in my life over the years. All of us possess gifts that we have repressed because of the different issues we have lived through. The Lord can break that hold, and we can experience a fuller understanding of just how many blessings God has given us as we use them to bless others in His name.

As soon as the new school year began, my parents surprised me with a new guitar. They had a miraculous few dollars that they used to buy a twelve-string Brazilian instrument. Their rationale was that if I indeed had developed a ministry, they wanted to help me succeed.

That Giannini Craviola guitar played for countless thousands of people around the world in the next fifteen years, always when I preached a sermon.

The day would come only three years later when I became a pastor, and then a couple years later, a youth specialist and evangelist. The time even came a few years after when I would work with the president of the United States.

You never can imagine what changes God can bring to your life, but you can discover them when you surrender your life to Him.

I think back to the day of those swarming blackbirds on my high school campus often and will always cherish that sunny day when I was sixteen. Little did I know that in giving my life to Jesus, a virtual avalanche would be set off; an avalanche of experiences of growth and change in my life. I am grateful to my friend Johnny Perez, who was faithful and stayed insistent with me until I saw the light before me. Johnny brought me to understand the power of a personal God. I changed from the "quiet" student on campus to a student with an attitude, the attitude of Jesus. It starts here, *ese* . . .

José Vicente Rojas serves as the Director of the Office of Volunteer Ministries for the North American Division. An accomplished musician and recording artist, José is also an author and a passionate preacher of the Word. José holds an Honoris Causa Doctor of Divinity degree from Southwestern Adventist University, as well as Bachelors and Masters degrees in Religion from Loma Linda University. He and his wife, Ruthie, have four children: Veronica, Angelica, Gabriel, and Maria.

BIG VISION AND ESCALATORS

José Cortés

WHEN I WOKE UP THAT COLD NOVEMBER morning in our sixth-floor apartment in Madrid, Spain, I felt different. As a kid, I had always wanted to be a doctor. My father had instilled in me and my brother the idea that being missionary doctors would be one of the best things we could do with our lives. Whenever someone asked, "What do you want to do with your life?" or "What do you want to be when you grow up?" I would always reply, "A missionary doctor." But at age fifteen, in what seemed like an overnight change, I had a different vision for my life.

That morning during family worship, I announced to my family that I no longer wanted to be a missionary doctor; I felt that God wanted me to be a pastor. My father, who is a pastor, was super-excited, and my mother and my brother also joined in with happiness. But there was Someone even more delighted with my announcement than were my parents and brother. I could imagine God jumping up for joy from His throne and excitedly clapping His holy hands at my announcement.

By now you are asking, "How do you know God did that?" Let me assure you, God celebrates whenever one of His children, whom He created with love, finds the purpose and the vision for his or her life. He loves it even more when we fulfill that vision with His blessing. God created you and me with awesome talents and gifts, and He surely gets excited as He watches us make choices and develop those gifts to fulfill an awesome vision. After all, He wants to bless you with a great present and an excellent future. " 'I know the plans I have for you,' declares the LORD, 'plans to prosper you and not to harm you, plans to give you hope and a future' " (Jeremiah 29:11, NIV).

HAVE A VISION

What is your purpose? Do you have a vision for your life? Perhaps we first need to know what vision is. My personal definition of *vision* is "the ability or power to see things that may happen, before they happen." It's like a dream or a goal of something that will one day occur. Vision is so important that without it, people, towns, cities, nations, and even churches cannot thrive and eventually cease to exist. The Bible says, "Where there is no vision, the people perish" (Proverbs 29:18, KJV).

A life without vision is like a day without sun, a car without wheels, a wedding without a bride, a family without love. It's like football without the Giants or baseball without the Yankees (at least for New Yorkers). A life without a vision is incomplete.

This is why I'd like to challenge you to take a deep breath, close your eyes for a few moments, and think about your life. Where are you headed? Where are you going to be next year? How about in five, ten, and twenty years from now? What legacy are you going to leave to those who will come after you? If you cannot see it, perhaps it will never be. Remarkable lives and achievements are most often the result of a vision, which was born first as a small thought in a person's mind. Close your eyes again and think. What do you see?

DREAM BIG

Do not be afraid to see something big and very remarkable. Don't hesitate in dreaming the impossible dream. After all, God's children are supposed to be the head and not the tail. Remember King David? He started out as a young man taking care of his father's sheep. His father, his brothers, and his pastor (the prophet Samuel) saw him as just a shepherd boy.

In their minds, David's legacy would have been that of a good man who took care of sheep all his life and then passed the trade on to his kids and grandkids. While others in the family and in the church were thinking *shepherd for life,* God was thinking *king for life.* While your parents, relatives, friends, and even church leaders may see you as a simple high-school student trying to graduate; a college student struggling with finances, midterms, and finals; a dropout with attention deficit disorder who cannot stay still for more than two minutes; or a college graduate who cannot find a job in his or her area. But God is thinking differently about you!

He is actually dreaming big. God is looking at you and envisioning a successful businesswoman who makes money and benefits the needy; a great father and loving husband; a caring mother with the best family ever; a missionary doctor who brings healing to thousands; a teacher who molds the lives of many kids; the pastor of a growing and active congregation who brings hope to a big city; the president of the Adventist Church in your region who leads with vision and integrity; a senator who actually legislates to benefit the people; or perhaps the first Adventist president of the United States.

If your vision for your life does not scare you, perhaps

it is not big enough. If others don't laugh at you or shake their heads in disbelief when you share your vision with them, perhaps you should reevaluate your vision. God is thinking great plans, an awesome future, and a life filled with purpose for you. Just don't be afraid to dream big!

OBSTACLES ARE THE ESCALATOR

Whenever you have a vision, be assured there will be obstacles. I must be candid with you. God wants to prosper and bless you, and as if that were not enough, He gives you eternal life. But there is someone else who wants exactly the opposite. Satan wants to spoil your plans, discredit you, make you miserable, and then kill you (1 Peter 5:8).

Satan does not want you to have a vision. He wants you to believe that you are mediocre and that all there is to life is struggle, addiction, debt, disease, injustice, and death. This is why, whenever you come up with a purpose and a vision for your life, Satan will try to discourage you—and he is pretty good at it. He is a pro at trying to discourage people with vision. He will use others, at times those closest to you—family, friends, colleagues,and even some in the church—who will become obstacles in the "name of God." Have you ever shared your dreams and plans with someone you love and trust, only to receive strange looks, comments about how impossible it is, laughter, and maybe some ridicule? The purpose and vision for your life usually come with obstacles. But remember there is a beautiful promise in the Bible: "I can do all things through Christ who strengthens me" (Philippians 4:13, NKJV).

When you are truly serious about your vision, the obstacles become your stepping-stones. They can stretch you and help you fulfill your vision. One day, when David was taking care of his father's sheep, a bear came and tried to steal one of the sheep; David fought the bear and killed it. On another day, a lion came with the same intent as the bear; David was ready to fight the lion because he had already fought a bear. Then the giant Goliath came, and David was not afraid because he had already killed a bear and a lion, and he was ready for a giant.

God's vision for David was not that he would kill the giant. God's vision for David was that he would be king; killing the giant was only a stepping-stone, as were protecting the sheep from the bear and the lion. When you have a vision, there will be obstacles, but you have the power of God in you. With the power of God, the obstacles that Satan puts in your way become the escalator to the fulfillment of your vision.

When I embraced God's vision for my life, I began

to work on it right away. Because my purpose was now to become a pastor who would minister to others with the hope of salvation, I started praying more, reading my Bible more, and listening to sermons on tapes (even though I didn't have CDs, MP3s, or iPods then).

There was one preacher whom I admired; his office was in the world headquarters of the Seventh-day Adventist Church in Maryland. He was very well known, regarded by many as a great evangelist. Now that I was living in the United States and in eleventh grade, I read about him in the Adventist magazines and at times heard his tapes.

Great was my joy when I heard that this man would be the evangelist at a series close to our home. I asked my father to take me with him so I could hear the preacher and perhaps meet him personally. I still remember the opening night, a packed auditorium, great and famous Adventist musicians—it was a wonderful atmosphere. The sermon was also very good.

Once the sermon was finished, my father and I went backstage. I really wanted to meet the preacher, whose name I won't mention. A long line of people were waiting to speak with him. Finally, it was my turn, and my father introduced me to the evangelist. He said, "This is my son, José; he wants to be a pastor."

I was excited because I admired this preacher, and

his worldwide appeal as an evangelist impressed me. As I shook his hand, he looked down at me and said, "You are too short to be a pastor." That was his reply! That was all he said. I wondered if the reply was a joke and was waiting for the punch line, but it never came. *He can't be serious, can he?* Well, he did look very serious to me and did not attempt to retract the statement.

I looked at my dad, my dad looked at me, and we walked away disappointed. I was really looking for some affirmation, as all sixteen-year-old teens do, but received criticism instead. I had been sure the man of God would affirm my desire to serve God, but he never did. Perhaps he simply saw a teen and did not acknowledge my vision. But God did.

By the way, God's plan can be pretty funny at times. Years passed, I finished high school, finished college, and the Potomac Conference of the Seventh-day Adventist Church hired me as a pastor. I was sent to the Adventist theological seminary to earn a master's degree. Then, after serving at several churches in the Washington, D.C., area, I was asked to become the pastor of the Silver Spring Spanish Seventh-day Adventist Church, right down the road from the world headquarters of the Seventh-day Adventist Church.

I still remember that Sabbath, when, at age twenty-six, I was installed as the pastor of the church in Silver

Spring. As I stood up to preach, I looked to my left, and guess who was sitting there? Yes, it was the very same famous evangelist who, ten years earlier, had told me that I was too short to be a pastor. God has a sense of humor. When you have a vision and a purpose for your life, there will be obstacles, but there is the power of God.

After the sermon, I stood by the central door of the church to greet people as they left. As the evangelist passed by, I realized that he was no longer very tall and was a bit hunched over; I could tell age had taken its toll on him. He greeted me as "Pastor." It felt so good to have that very same pastor who had once told me I was too short to be a pastor now calling me "Pastor." I quickly decided to treat him with love and respect. We chatted a little bit, and during the conversation he told me, "I am retiring soon. The brethren [referring to the leadership at the world headquarters] think it is time for me to hang up my gloves, but when you go out of town and need someone to preach for you, remember me. I am here for you."

Take a moment right now and ask God to give you that vision for your life. I expect to see and hear great things from you in the days, months, and years to come. If you already have that vision, ask God to strengthen it. And please remember, there will be obstacles, but with the power of God, the obstacles become simple escalators and in some cases elevators. Whoever you may be today, there's no telling how God can change you and make you into an instrument of service.

José H. Cortés Jr., MA, was born in Cuba and has served as a pastor and youth director since 1992. He recently became the Youth Director of the Atlantic Union Conference. He and his wife, Joanne, have two children: José Herminio III and Joel Benjamin. He is presently pursuing a Doctor of Ministry degree.

WHAT SHOULD I DO?

CARLOS A. CAMACHO

HERE I AM ONCE AGAIN, WITH THE OLD FAMILIAR feeling. I feel like the old-school rapper Hi-C with his, "What shall I, what shall I, what shall I do, sitting in the park waiting for you." But seriously though, what should I do? Should I just start working, or should I go to school? If I go to school, it's going to be really tough; my parents don't have any money and I don't even have financial aid. I could really help my parents if I got a little job somewhere and started making some money. What should I do? Those were the choices I faced in my teenage years.

Another game of pros and cons, an overwhelming feeling of uncertainty that keeps me up at night; I just want to do the right thing! I wish someone would just come and tell me exactly what to do! I need to make a decision. I hate being here. I want to close my eyes and wake up the moment after the decision is made. Wouldn't that be nice?

How do you make up your mind about things? How do you make wise decisions? Are there any tools or tricks to help us make the right decision? Are some people simply smarter than the rest of us, so they make wiser decisions than we do?

We make decisions every day and every minute. We begin making decisions the moment we wake up in the morning, all day long, and down to the last second before we go to sleep at night. Some of the decisions are conscious, but many aren't. As soon as we wake up, we must quickly decide to either get up out of bed or sleep for just another "five minutes." Been there?

All decisions have something in common: they will be made. You either make the decision, or someone else will. When a decision you were supposed to make isn't made and something or someone else makes it for you, you lose control of your life. The more decisions you make, the more you are in control of your life.

The opposite of being in control is to become a victim of your circumstances, and you don't want that, especially for long periods of time. Jails, hospitals, and cemeteries are not just full of people who made wrong decisions but with people who didn't exercise their God-given right to make their own decisions. Someone else did it for them, and they ended up at a place they didn't want to be.

Jails are places where most of the decision making is stripped away from the individual. Human beings were made to be free and to enjoy their freedom to choose and to make their own decisions. Life is all about freedom— freedom to make decisions. Being incarcerated is the opposite. In jail, your decision making is reduced to almost nothing. Our minds were made to be decisive, and the more we practice, the better we become at decision making.

MAKING WISE DECISIONS

I particularly don't believe that whole idea of playing "guessing games" with God. Some people think that God has this one perfect way your life should be, and it's up to you to guess your way through life to find it. I don't think so. Life is much more complicated, and God is much more loving than that.

The God who made you also equipped you with a marvelous brain, with certain capacities that often-times we don't know about or understand. You make decisions every single day of your life. You either decided to read this book or someone else did it for you. You are capable of making decisions. The question is not whether you can or can't make decisions. I'm telling you, you can and you do. The question is, are those decisions that you're making wise decisions? Are they giving you a better life—or bringing you pain and brokenness? Are they decisions that you're making for the long run—or just for momentary pleasure?

One of the decisions I made early in my adolescence was to remain a virgin for marriage. Call me stupid if you will, but I still believe it's one of the coolest decisions I've ever made.

It all started with a mom who kept pressing on me the need to respect women, partly by reminding me I had three sisters to help protect. So early on and before those teenage urges got the best of me, I made my decision to remain pure for marriage. I would simply pray about it and ask God to help me.

One time, knowingly, I allowed myself into a situation that quickly got out of hand. I soon realized it's far easier to make rational decisions when you have all your blood in your brain as opposed to when most of the blood is elsewhere! Confession time: in the heat of the moment, I gave up.

Suddenly, all I cared for was the so-called reward my normal physical body was ready for. My abstinence decision was completely overshadowed by passion and desire. I was done. But God wasn't.

I didn't have sex that evening. And although things happened that I'm not proud of, I was able to remain a virgin till I got married. And the question is, Was I able to do that on my own? Am I that good and a better-than-thou Christian? No, I'm not.

It was *not* that I was able to overcome because of my extraordinary willpower—God knows that I would be skinny if I had any willpower! It was all God. He comes through even when we won't or can't. What happened to me was all based on God's willingness to honor a decision I made way before I got into that situation.

When you make a decision based on principle before God, He will see you through it. He honors your decisions by giving you the ability to remain faithful, and if you fail (because life isn't perfect and sometimes we do mess up!), He still gives you the ability to get up again and keep on trying. "Take delight in the LORD, and he will give you the desires of your heart" (Psalm 37:4, NIV).

God loves you and wants you to truly enjoy every aspect of your life and every stage of your growth and experience; He loves you that much!

There are all kinds of decisions. Some are easy, others are pretty hard. Some are mundane while many are eternal. Decisions decide our future, whether eternal or not. Should you buy a green dress or a blue one? Should you play PSP or Xbox 360? Does it even matter? Nevertheless, these are decisions you may need to make.

There are other types of decisions such as, should

you join the soccer team at school when you know they play on Sabbath, the day you keep as God's holy day? Should you go to the church teen camp, or should you stay home and go to the teen dance party over the weekend? Those are harder decisions because they can potentially affect the direction of your life.

What about this one: your friend tells you she's thinking about having an abortion. She's trying to find a "quick fix" to mend a poor choice she made; she's trying to avoid all the drama. After all, she's just a young, unmarried teenager, the father has bailed, and the last thing on her mind is to become a young single parent. What would you tell her?

If you tell her what you both know is the right thing to do, it's probably *not* what she wants to hear. She could have gone to her mom for that! So what do you say? What do you do in such a situation?

For some people there's not even a choice to be made because they feel abortion is not the answer. We try hard to convince ourselves and others that it's better for all concerned to just get the abortion, when it's not! All the signs point to that "easy" way out. Trying to decide between good and bad is really not that hard, and yet, for many uninformed teens, it's such a hard decision to be made that some have taken their lives instead of working through the problem and facing the consequences.

Other kinds of decisions are pretty tough because they are deceiving in nature. They seem not to have much to do with good and evil but rather with the direction our lives are to take: the career you're supposed to pursue; the person you're supposed to marry; the level of importance that God and the church will have in your life.

As far as I'm concerned, those are tough because they look pretty innocent—but they are most important. The career you decide to pursue will affect your life for the future. The person you marry will end up having more influence in your life than your decision to remain in the church. Taking a test on Sabbath or going to games you feel you need to go to are the kind of decisions that will outline your path in the long run.

There are three steps that will help give you perspective when it comes to making wise decisions in a godly manner. You'll need wisdom, willingness, and work.

WISDOM

Some decisions are hard right off the bat. As soon as you recognize it, you're asking your friends and loved ones to help you out. Good for you; that's what friends are for, right? But let me suggest something: why not ask the manufacturer of the product? Why not ask the

One who made you? Why not ask Him who knows the future as clearly as you know the past? Ask God!

The Bible says all real wisdom comes from God. King Solomon gives you this advice:

> These are the wise sayings of Solomon,
>   David's son, Israel's king—
> Written down so we'll know how to live well
>   and right,
>   to understand what life means and where it's
>   going;
> A manual for living,
>   for learning what's right and just and fair;
> To teach the inexperienced the ropes
>   and give our young people a grasp on reality
>   (Proverbs 1:1–4, *The Message*).

Isn't that pretty cool? Did you catch the flow of what the wisest man who ever lived is telling you? God can make you wise! God can help you out as you attempt to make decisions! In the same chapter, Solomon says,

> Start with GOD—the first step in learning is
>   bowing down to GOD;
>   only fools thumb their noses at such wisdom
>   and learning.

Pay close attention, friend, to what your father
     tells you;
     never forget what you learned at your mother's
         knee.
Wear their counsel like flowers in your hair,
     like rings on your fingers (verses 7–9, *The
         Message*).

So now, Solomon throws in the trilogy of people to counsel with: God, your father, and your mother. I know you may be missing one or two out of the three; nevertheless, you still have God and maybe other father and mother figures you can go to. Take advantage of that.

Solomon seems to know what's going on nowadays when he talks about peer pressure and other things in the following verses:

Dear friend, if bad companions tempt you,
     don't go along with them.
If they say—"Let's go out and raise some hell.
     Let's beat up some old man, mug some old
         woman.
Let's pick them clean
     and get them ready for their funerals.
We'll load up on top-quality loot.
     We'll haul it home by the truckload.

Join us for the time of your life!
      With us, it's share and share alike!"—
Oh, friend, don't give them a second look;
      don't listen to them for a minute.
They're racing to a very bad end,
      hurrying to ruin everything they lay hands on.
Nobody robs a bank
      with everyone watching,
Yet that's what these people are doing—
      they're doing themselves in.
When you grab all you can get, that's what
            happens:
      the more you get, the less you are (verses
      10–19, *The Message*).

I love the part where he levels with you and says, "Oh, friend, don't give them a second look; don't listen to them for a minute. They're racing to a very bad end, hurrying to ruin everything they lay hands on." Anyway, when you need to make a decision, come to God and ask for wisdom. He's always willing to share with you and help you out.

WILLINGNESS

You need to be willing to live with the fact that frequently the best decisions in life are neither popular or pleasant. Sometimes the best decision will generate some heat and cause you some pain. This world is not necessarily keen on best decisions. If you have decided to remain a virgin, then someone will think you're just gay. If you decide not to join a gang or a certain group of "friends" at school, there's probably a price you'll pay for that, but the right decision will reward you in the long run.

When you become convicted of something and you are willing to stand by it, people usually get it after a while, even if they don't buy it. As you attempt to make a decision, think about the consequences and ask yourself if you're willing to live with them.

Revolutionary Jesus knew that giving His life for us sinners wasn't going to be easy or popular. Not even His disciples understood or appreciated what He was doing at the time, but boy, was that a good decision! Let me tell you, that was the best decision God and Jesus ever made for us! It gave us the opportunity to be made right with God. But it came with a huge price tag. The best decisions are often costly, but in the long run they'll give you life—eternal life, that is.

WAIT

One of the traits of people who have an especially hard time making decisions is that they'll prolong making a decision as much as possible in hopes they don't have to make it at all. I know people who have lost their marriages over their inability to make decisions. Solomon also said there is a time for everything. Wait just long enough.

When it comes to making an important decision, you certainly don't want to jump right into the decision without giving it some thought. But by the same token, the time will come for you to make that decision, and you must. As I said before, if you don't make the decision, someone else will make it for you, and chances are, you won't like it!

The period of waiting can either be devastating or uplifting. If you just sit there and let worry take the best out of you or play all the worst-case scenarios in your head over and over, you'll drive yourself crazy! The waiting period is the opportunity you have to pray, to ask people whom you hold in high regard (parents, pastors, mentors, teachers, adult friends whom you trust, and so on) help you look at the pros and cons, and finally make your decision.

In my experience, most of the important decisions I've made have not been easy. I would be lying if I were to tell you that after taking those steps, I knew just what to do. It has actually been more like: "OK, Lord, this is what I think is right based on my understanding of Your desire for my life, and here's what I'm going to do. Nevertheless, You have the last word, so do what You have to do if You desire something different; but as for me, I've decided to go in this direction."

In my case, the assurance comes after the fact, and that is fine with me. You may experience something different, and that is fine too. The idea is to take your time and do what you have to do. Although you're not to rush into anything, don't give up your right or opportunity to make a decision by prolonging it indefinitely.

SUBCONSCIOUS DECISIONS

More and more scientists have discovered that conscious decision making that involves rational thinking and other mental activities is far less accurate than subconscious decision making. This groundbreaking discovery shows that when the brain has the right kind of information, our subconscious state has the power to make the right decision even before we reason or think about it.

People have called this the gut instinct; I would rather call it the Spirit of God working in your life even at subconscious levels. The trick is feeding your brain the right kind of information. I'm not going to preach right here about the evils of television, video games, and music, but I will remind you that the brain God gave you is like an empty warehouse, and you get to fill it up with whatever you want.

I invite you to fill up your brain with the good stuff, so that your decision making will be easier, so that the right kind of information will lead you to doing what is right, and your reasoning and thought processes can lead you to the cross of Jesus.

Have you made some poor decisions in your life? Are you paying the consequences? An wanted pregnancy, the use of narcotics, an incomplete education, maybe hanging out with the wrong crowd? God can *change* that. In fact, God keeps changing you every minute. You and I know there is no way we can go back into the past and change things, but we can surely make better decisions in the present and for the future—and that's where God can help.

Being a teenager is not an easy thing, especially because this is the time when you make choices that will be with you for the rest of your life. Don't be scared, though; you're not alone. There's a whole gang of people willing and able to help you, and there's God especially—God who loves you unconditionally.

God takes you just as you are because He has the power to change you into something beautiful and very much worthwhile. I know, sometimes it's hard to believe, and we ignore that fact and keep on going solo.

God made a decision a long time ago: He decided to stick with you through thick and thin, to take you with Him, and invite you to spend eternity with Him. He's done everything in His power, and now He's given you a choice: will you let Him change you? He's made His choice, will you?

By the way, to finish the story I started with: I did both. I went to school, and I worked hard. I washed cars, planted pine trees in the freezing cold, waited tables, and cooked at restaurants. But after seven years, I was able to finish a four-year degree. Later, I did a master's degree. I look back and all I can say is, "Thank You, God, for being there in my decision making. Thank You for Your ever-present desire to change us into something useful for Your kingdom." May God be glorified in your life story.

Carlos A. Camacho, MA, Director of Sales and Marketing at Pacific Press and the compiler and the person responsible for the Changed series. He's passionate about preaching the Word of God to youth and beyond. He and his wife, Samantha, have two children: Samuel and Carly, and have a third one on the way. His personal preaching motto is, "To bring comfort to the afflicted and affliction to the comforted."

DATING: ASKING THE BIG QUESTION

CARLOS ACOSTA

DO YOU WANT TO BE MY LADY?" I ASKED HER ON that unforgettable night. I had finally built up enough courage to pop the big question to this beautiful young woman I had befriended for months. I was sweating, and my heart was pounding so hard I felt it would jump out of my chest. I had prepared all day long in front of the mirror. Would she say Yes? Would she tell me, "I'll think about it"? I had a pretty good idea that she would say Yes, but I still wasn't 100 percent sure.

I had a bouquet of red roses for the occasion. *These will definitely help me!* I told myself. I was ready. My pants were sharply creased, my shirt ironed, my hair just right, and the last of my cheap college cologne sprayed on me. We met in one of the gardens at the Adventist university where we were studying in Mexico. I asked her if she wanted to be my girl, the one and only for me. As I stood there waiting for the answer, before she said anything, her eyes said it all. On that August night in 1997, Alma said Yes! to me. It was the beginning of something very special.

A PROMISE AND A PRAYER

In August 1996, at age twenty-one, I was a student at the theological seminary, and I made a very important dating decision. I decided that I would not play with the feelings of any young woman I met from that point on. I decided that I would not mislead anyone into thinking that we could have a special relationship if I was not going to be serious about it. I decided I was not going to break my heart or anyone else's. I decided that instead of being a flirt, I would have friends. I made a prayer request that day to God: "I ask that You lead my life as a single person. I ask that You help me in the dating decisions I make. God, I want to have only one girlfriend, and when that happens, I would like her to be my future wife. I trust that You will lead me. Amen!" I was looking to not do my will when it came to dating but to do His will.

I made that decision because I had been in the dating scene since age thirteen, and up to that moment of my prayer, every dating experience had ended in two broken hearts. I recalled my dating days as a single man before becoming a Christian. Like most everyone else, I was in trial-and-error mode when it came to dating. It had been a disaster. All I could remember was leaving a trail of broken hearts and tears. One of those disastrous experiences was when I was a gangbanger, and I met a young woman who I thought "loved" me. I was so much into her that I tattooed her name on my arm! It ended when I found her with another guy. I burned her name off. Ouch!

Then I became a Christian. After being in a major street gang in L.A. from an early age, I found Jesus when I was nineteen, and my life did a 180-degree turn. When I was settled into my new life, I started to date again. I began to meet young women from church as I began to go to Bible studies, youth camps, and social activities. These girls were great! They were much different from others I had met before. I thought to myself, *Dating in the church will be different.* It certainly was different, but my first two experiences ended with hearts being broken also. I asked myself, "Is there a better way to date? How can I avoid these heartaches and disappointments as a single guy?" The answer eventually came. I experienced a better way of approaching the dating scene. This better way would turn out to be one of the biggest blessings I could experience as a single young man.

THE BETTER WAY OF DATING

First, the better way of dating began with what is in me. My attitudes and thinking about dating had to change. The models I was following were models that I had either grown up with or I had seen other friends experience. I made the decision to stop misleading myself and young women. I would no longer jump into a relationship to "experience" or "see" and then step out if I didn't like it. From then on, I would respect young women's feelings and, above all, respect them as daughters of God. Messing with their feelings and breaking their hearts was something I sensed God did not appreciate me doing.

Second, the better way of dating is a series of proven steps, tactics that are common sense when put into practice by anyone who is ready to date. Many have benefited from following this way of dating, including me. They are laid out for you here in five steps.

FRIENDS FIRST, DATE LATER

In my first year of my bachelor's degree in theology, I began to meet many female friends. At that time, the University of Montemorelos, a Christian Adventist school in northern Mexico, had a ratio of two women for every man on campus. I had just arrived from Los Angeles, and I was amazed. It was every single man's dream come true! As soon as I began my classes, I began to assimilate into student life, getting to know people. The possibilities to date came up. But in every opportunity I would think about my prayer and the promise I had made to God. On many occasions I had to restrain my feelings and desires for dating a particular young woman. I could foresee the bad outcome. It was very tough.

Instead, I became friends in the full sense of the word. Even though there was a mutual likeability, I would not allow my feelings to get the best of me. I would be friends, with no interest at all other than being friends. That personal policy kept my brain working and my eyes open, and it made me more capable of rational decisions. If I were approached by any of my female friends, I would still hold myself accountable to my own policy. I would not mislead anyone. I would proceed only if I sensed that God wanted me to.

During the first year of school, I met Alma, the girl who eventually said Yes! to me. I met her at one of the university's social activities. We quickly became friends. There was something very special and different about her. We were friends for eight months. During those eight months, my personal policy stayed in place. I really liked her, I was attracted to her, but I would not give her false hope. During those eight months, we hung out mostly with a group of friends and very few times alone. We both kept our other friends, and we were able to go in and out of our circle of friends without a problem. Our mutual friendship grew, and we both sensed that we could have something special. That was eventually confirmed by our circle of friends too. But a lot was on the line. I would not give Alma false hopes or mess around with her feelings if I was not sure about a serious relationship with her.

My main purpose at this stage was to finish my college studies. My focus was mainly on my classes, my grades, and my life. Even though Alma and I were friends, everything was focused on achieving the goal of graduating with a four-year college degree. We spoke a lot about our individual dreams, which included postgraduate studies in the U.S. for me, and the same for her in Mexico. We encouraged each other in our studies and in our dreams.

READY, SET, DATE

After much prayer, I decided I was ready to proceed to the next step: dating Alma. This was the first time after months of friendship that I asked her out. For the first time, we both stepped out of our groups of friends and began to spend more time exclusively with each other. We began to go out on dates to restaurants, the movies, plays, concerts, and so on. As we kept spending more time with each other, mutual feelings of romance began to increase. Still, my policy of not misleading was in place. We both knew that we were really attracted to each other. She didn't want to risk having her feelings hurt, and I didn't want to either.

Also, at this stage of our relationship, I met her parents. I felt that I had a responsibility to ask her parents for permission every time we would go out on a date. I thought that they needed to be part of this period too. I asked them what their thinking about dating was and what hours were appropriate for me to bring Alma back home at night. Her parents in return asked me many questions about who I was, who my parents were, what my beliefs were, and what I was studying. Now, in the past, I would have been uncomfortable with all the questions and with the fact that her parents had to approve of our going out. But not anymore. I thanked God for the chance of getting to know Alma's parents and making them part of the dating process. I was very happy to inform them where we were going, who we were going with, and what time we planned to return.

The dating was exciting! We spent lots of time getting to know each other better. We talked about Alma's dream of being a nutritionist and how she wanted to open her own chain of restaurants and buy a house for her parents. She was a hairstylist, too, and she dreamed of owning a beauty salon and was saving money for that. I was happy to hear about her dreams, and I supported them.

Dating became an opportunity for getting to know each other deeper and better. It was spent on going places but above all talking about each other's dreams and future plans.

COURTSHIP: WANT TO BE MY GIRLFRIEND?

Sounds cheesy, right? But that's how it was. After we had been friends, after dating, and after much praying, I was ready to take the next step: asking her to be my girlfriend. By this time, I wasn't thinking on how "good" or how "cute" we would look together. I was thinking about the prayer I had made to God. Before making the decision, I remembered that I had asked Him that the girl who would become my girlfriend would eventually be my wife. I was thinking about the future and about a possible commitment and responsibility. My love for her was there, and it was deep. I had gotten to know her well during our friendship stage and during the dating. Our relationship kept growing. My next step carried with it the possibility of this relationship going into marriage. It was a possibility that I wanted and that I was seeking.

After getting through the big "Yes! I want to be your girlfriend" decision, we went to Alma's parents. I wanted to ask her parents' permission too. When I showed up at their house, her dad and mom sat me down in the living room and asked, "What is it that you want to talk to us about?"

I was very nervous, my mouth was dry, and the words would not come out! Her dad was the one who spoke the words I needed to say, and they gave us their approval. We were officially a courting couple.

During the next two and a half years, our courting relationship grew. Our main focus was still our college degrees and knowing each other more. We did not speak about marriage for at least the first two years! Not that I didn't think about it. We didn't have to speed up our relationship. We only had to pace it. It was more like taking a cruise in a car and not a high-speed chase. We got to do more things together, and we enjoyed each other's company very much. Another thing that helped us to take it easy was our parents. They constantly reminded us, "First finish what you came to do here, which is to graduate, and then you two can think about marriage." So we did.

A very important help to us as a courting couple was our relationship with Jesus. We both were Christians and both prayed, and we read the Bible individually and together as a couple. We also attended the university church, where we were both involved in many of its activities. I was a deacon and director of the prison ministry; she was a Sabbath School assistant and was also a singer in a Christian group. Being active in our faith really helped us, and I believe it brought us closer to each other. Our faith also helped us to keep God in the middle of every decision we had to take as a courting couple.

Neither of us in any way discouraged the other's dreams and objectives, even if it meant separating and studying or working apart from each other. I never felt an ownership over her, nor in any way did I impose on or destroy her personal dreams.

Another thing that we both agreed as a Christian couple to do was to set limits on our physical contact and in regard to sex. This obviously was very difficult but not impossible to do. I'll explain why and how.

One of the dangers of any courting couple is not setting limits on physical contact. By not doing that, you are leaving open a path that eventually leads to sex. Many young people believe that once you have a "Yes! I want to be your girlfriend or boyfriend," that this in itself gives them permission to kiss and touch as much as one likes. It's a big mistake! Many young people go into relationships just because of that. Not having limits on physical contact will blur the most important thing a courting couple must do during that period, which is get to know each other. Young couples today are more focused on the physical side of the relationship, and everything else gets put on the back burner. A courting couple must be focused on learning more about each other and getting to know the other person better instead of "feeling" each other's bodies. Many courting couples who spend too much time on the physical are blinded to the negative character traits and habits of the other person. Many come to discover the negatives when it's too late.

One of the things that Alma and I did to set limits in our physical contact was never to be home alone. Alma was living with her parents, and I was living with my roommates off campus. Every time I went to pick her up (I didn't have a car, just a bicycle), I would stay outside the gate or the door. Every time she swung by my apartment, she would stay outside the door! My college roommates and I established a rule that no women besides our moms would enter the apartment. And if someone was found to have broken the rule, we would have a serious conversation with him. My roommates helped a lot.

Another thing that helped Alma and me to keep our limits was the fact that we were both studying in a Christian university. You would not believe this, but physical contact between courting couples was not allowed! We could not walk around the halls hugging each other or even holding hands. Being caught kissing was a definite no-no. Now, me being from Los Angeles, did I believe that these rules were too much for me? No! Where I come from, there were no rules when it came to dating. Growing up in the barrios of East Los Angeles, West Los Angeles, and Compton, it was pretty much open season. I had dated in L.A., and my models for behavior were what I saw where I lived. My growing up in my early and late teen years was filled with friends' pregnancies, STDs, AIDS, shacking up, divorce, and worse. Now, suddenly, I found myself in a world where there were rules about dating, a world where parents' counsels were taken into consideration, and rules were set to protect a courting couple and a potential future marriage. I had no problem with that. I understood that rules, especially when it came to dating and courting, were there to protect my girlfriend and me.

A quick observation: It's in this stage that many courting couples have to also be aware of the "check engine light" and take the relationship to the mechanic shop or the junkyard. Warning signs that you should not ignore are cheating, addictions, dependency ("I can't live without you! I'll die if you leave me!"), and physical or emotional abuse. If you don't deal with them at this stage, they will deal with you later on—and you will regret it.

Was our courtship relationship easy all the time? No, it was not. We had a couple of breakups that helped us to evaluate our relationship. Those moments were very sad but helpful, as they gave us the opportunity to change things that needed to be changed. I thanked God that our relationship became stronger after these periods of evaluation.

I HEAR THE BELLS!

After two years of courtship, we spoke about the possibility of marriage. We decided to move toward marriage for many reasons. Our love was strong, my graduation was a year away, and once I graduated, I would be able to meet the responsibility that comes with marriage. We had tested our feelings during the courtship, and they had remained consistent. I knew I wanted to be with Alma for the rest of my life.

So I proposed marriage to her on a Saturday night after church services. I arranged a nice dinner in the university gardens and had a bunch of my friends from the seminary come and play Mexican serenades. A friend of mine picked up Alma and brought her to the surprise dinner I had prepared for her. I welcomed her by singing a special serenade song. Then I knelt and asked her if she wanted to be my wife. Again, she said Yes! Touchdown, baby!

This time we decided to share the news with both sets of parents. I called my parents and told them that I needed them to come and visit. I would ask for Alma's hand in marriage. (Not that I wanted to marry her hand; I wanted to marry her!) My parents were in Denver, Colorado, at the time, and they drove to the university. Alma and I also spoke to her parents, and her parents agreed to our marriage with one condition, that I would graduate first and Alma would finish her college degree after we married.

The date was set, and we were just a few months away. We were happy. One of our first priorities was to take a premarital counseling course with a spiritual mentor at the university. It helped us to fast-forward to married life and showed us how to deal with obstacles that every young married couple faces. The mentor was very helpful, and he was there every step of the way.

At this stage of our relationship, we were pretty sure we wanted to marry. In my case, I had no interest in any other young women besides Alma. I was convinced not only by her looks but by her character, her way of thinking, her way of dealing with problems, and many other things. Our conversations were not only from the heart but also from the mind. During this time, she was still probing the idea of whether I was the right person for her too! I'm glad I passed the test.

Finally, prayer was key in our decision to proceed toward marriage. My fiancée and I read a book titled *The Adventist Home,* and we found a very helpful quote which we put into practice at this stage. It reads, "If men and women are in the habit of praying twice a day before they contemplate marriage, they should pray four times a day when such a step is anticipated. Marriage is something that will influence and affect your life, both in this world and in the world to come."[1] We prayed, prayed, and prayed some more, seeking God's approval for this final step. After much prayer, we both sensed that it was the right thing to do.

I graduated with my bachelor's degree in theology six months before our wedding day. I had to give a year of service as a missionary and ended up going to southern Mexico. During the six months Alma and I were apart, and with many opportunities for either of us to walk away from the relationship and cancel the wedding, our love grew even stronger. This was the final test of our relationship.

Wedding day? Let's do this!

WEDDING DAY

On December 10, 2000, Alma and I got married.

After eight months of being friends and three years of courtship, the big day came. I had just finished my sixth month as a missionary and came back to the university for the wedding.

We had a simple wedding. We had only a hundred guests, and our mentor who took us through premarital counseling was the pastor who officiated at the wedding.

Alma looked beautiful in that white wedding dress, and I wasn't looking bad at all either in my black penguin suit. As her dad walked her down the aisle, my heart was beating with excitement. *This is the woman of my dreams, this is the woman I want to spend the rest of my life with,* I told myself. Another thought was, *I hope the pastor doesn't take long on his sermon. Let's get this over with!*

In the crowd I saw both sets of parents. I was happy to honor them by bringing Alma to the altar that day and receiving God's blessing for our marriage. Their approval of our relationship was as important as getting God's blessing. As we stood before the pastor and as he was asking us to repeat the wedding vows, I knew that God had answered my prayer for help to find the right girl for my life. He did it! I was staring at her beautiful eyes through that white veil as we both knelt.

After our wedding, we left for our honeymoon in Cancun, Mexico. For that to happen, I had sold my little Toyota. After our honeymoon, we went to live in

Merida, Yucatan, where I had six more months to serve as a missionary. At the end of my service, we returned to the University of Montemorelos, but now as a married couple. I began my master's degree in family relations, and Alma continued her studies as I promised her parents. She graduated with a bachelor's degree in elementary education.

ELEVEN YEARS AND COUNTING

We've been married for eleven years as I write this. We also have two beautiful daughters, Emily and Karlamichelle. I can tell you with a big smile that God has blessed our marriage. Did this happen through good luck? No. We trace it back to a path that we both decided to follow as soon as we were friends, which continued during our dating, through our courtship, and finally to our wedding. It was a path that included God, prayer, clear thinking, self-discipline, lots of fun, and parents and mentors who helped us every step of the way.

I am writing to those who are single now, when there's a high rate of divorce, unwanted pregnancy, premarital sex, STDs, and couples who shack up and don't marry. Today, when the common belief among singles is that marriage "doesn't work anymore," I would like for you to avoid being among the statistics, among those whose hearts are broken in the jungle of dating.

If you're beginning to look around, and you're checking the scene to begin dating, pause and check your attitudes and your thinking about this. Are you ready to date? Will you be responsible with your feelings and with those of others? Ask yourself, "What model of dating will I follow? Does it help for me to have God in mind as I begin to date?" Answering these questions will be the keys to opening one of the most exciting experiences of your life.

If you've already been in the dating scene for a while, and if your heart has been broken a few times, or if you've been scarred by bad decisions, I invite you to pause and think. Ask yourself, "What attitudes and thoughts about dating do I need to change?" If you want changes for the better in future dating, change has to start with you right now! That's what I did. I had to stop and, with God's help, adopt a better way of dating that has resulted in my happiness and in a great relationship that I still enjoy today. I pray that it will be the same for you.

"Remember now your Creator in the days of your youth" (Ecclesiastes 12:1, NKJV).

---

1. Ellen G. White, *The Adventist Home* (Nashville: Southern Publishing, 1952), 71.

Carlos Acosta, MA, is the sole pastor of the Baldwin Park Bilingual Seventh-day Adventist Church in the Los Angeles area. He holds a BA in Theology and a MA degree in Family Relations and has a certification in drug addiction. He grew up in the barrios of L.A. and that's where he's chosen to serve God. He's married to Alma and has two beautiful children.

SEX

THE GOOD, THE BAD, AND THE UGLY

WILLY RAMOS

I LOVE YOU, *BOO-BOO*," I SAID AS SHE SMACKED ME IN my face. "Why are you doing this?" I asked again. "I love you! I'm not the one who raped you." This experience happened years ago while dating one of my now ex-girlfriends. She used me as a punching bag because she had been raped years earlier, and subconsciously she was determined to make all men pay.

And, even worse than that, she thought she had to have sex with me in order to prove her love. Like the time she surprised me on Valentine's Day when I showed up on her doorstep. She opened the door, to my surprise wearing nothing but some Victoria's Secret negligee and high heels. I pulled a Joseph and ran (I wouldn't be writing this down if I hadn't!). Satan still achieved at least one of his purposes. He knew I was going to photograph her half naked in my mind. I've been fighting to delete that image from my memory ever since.

I guess now is the time when I could say, in the words of that old-school female rap group Salt-n-Pepa, "Let's talk about sex, baby!"

I heard a pastor say this about sex once: "Sex is one of the best gifts God gave a married man." Then one of the parishioners said, "Yeah, and it's one of the worst curses the devil has given us single men." Wow, a gift or a curse? I guess it depends on how you look at it—or should I say, the way we live our lives?

Didn't God make sex so married couples could enjoy each other and procreate? Yes. He told Adam and Eve in the Garden, "Go get your *freak on,* and have babies!" (see Genesis 1:28). Have you ever thought that if it wasn't for sex we would have never been here? That means, ever since God gave the order, people have been getting *freaky*! (That sounds kinda gross, huh? My wife just asked me, "Why are you blushing?") So, what's the problem?

One of the problems is that we have corrupted sex. We have taken what God intended to be good and turned it bad, or ugly.

Did you know that when married couples have sex, angels of heaven surround their beds?[1] Yuck! When I first read that, I was like "*Ewwww!* Get outta here, you psychos," as I covered up my man-breast. That sounds a little disturbing, but putting high school humor aside, if that is true, then sex is an act of worship.

Can I tell you a secret? You promise you won't tell *La Junta* (the infamous church board)? My wife and I prayed on our honeymoon before we *did it*. I mean, it wasn't like one of those long, prayer warrior's fifteen-minute prayers! No way! I had business to attend to. It was more like a one-liner. A Marvin Gaye, "Let's get it on!" type joint! But we wanted God's blessing even in that.

So, hold up. Wait a minute. If God's holy angels surround your bed chambers when you're getting *freaky deaky*, that also means that Satan's angels or demons are by your side when you are *getting it on* in the back seat of your car or the hotel room or at your parents' house when they are not home.

You see, God has given us the privilege and the honor to procreate, to make babies. In doing so, we share the feeling Jesus felt when He created Adam and Eve. So the enemy is mad! In fact, really mad! An angel was not given that right. So what does he do? He tries to corrupt the awesome gift of God and to paint an ugly picture of it. That's why it's even a taboo subject in almost *all* our churches!

Example: When my wife and I go out on a date, I usually open the door for her and, when we are at a restaurant, pull out her chair so she can sit down. My father done raised me right! But I have an old-school Cadillac. I don't have the luxury of having an "open and close locks" thingy on my key chain. (My wife just told me they're called *keyless entry,* though *thingy* sounds better!) Also, my passenger side door does not have a keyhole to unlock it. So if old people or romantics see me walking my wifey to the car and getting inside first, while she waits outside for me to unlock her door, they would swear I was a jerk. And that I had no class at all.

But I'm not, for reals! I give her a box of half-eaten chocolates all the time! I just happen to look bad to the person who doesn't know better. And that's the same with sex. To the person who is ignorant of what God has to say about the matter, it could be perceived as bad; but for those who understand God's Word, sex is intended to be awesome, but only after you get married.

Did you know that the Bible talks a lot about sex? It does! (I can see some perverts searching the Scriptures as we speak. Me too! When I first found that out, I was a Bible thumper!)

Yo, have you ever read the *Song of Solomon*? What? That dude was *freak nasty*! In chapter 7 he says, "Girl, you got cute feet!" (see Song of Solomon 7:1). (So, brother had a foot fetish!) Then he talks about her legs, and her belly button (see verses 1, 2). (*Ooooooooh,* I'm-a tell your mama!) And last but certainly not least, he talks about her (wait . . . for . . . it . . .) *boobies*! Yup! Her breasts! He even says he's gonna grab them! (see verses 7, 8). Ha! Playa, playa! Wow, so God inspired King Solomon to write about breasts, legs, and thighs! (Sounds more like he was looking at a KFC menu! Ha!) You see, sex *is* good if God kept it in the Bible. We are the ones who made it bad.

When I got baptized eleven years ago, I became a born-again virgin. It's no secret. I have shared that in the pulpit many times. One day when one of my exes came to me and said, "I don't know why, but I haven't gotten my period," I wasn't afraid, not one bit. Why? Because I knew I never *hit that*! You see, there's freedom in doing things right and following God's plan for your life. You don't have to be worried that you're going to end up pregnant in high school. You don't have to worry if you're gonna end up with some kind of disease. Not to mention the emotional baggage you'll be free from carrying. For that reason alone you should hold out, because sometimes the emotional is way worse than the physical.

I know a girl who had two abortions. The first one was at the age of fourteen. Now she's like twenty. She tells me every year around the time the babies would have had their birthdays, she'll get so depressed that she locks herself in her room and cries herself to sleep at night. She quotes the prophet and says that before *them* babies were born, God knew them by name (Jeremiah 1:5). "And I murdered them," she says, *"I murdered them!"*

She has to live with the guilt that she killed her unborn kids because she and her boy just wanted to get their *freak on* when they were younger; to top it all off, she's not even with the *dude* anymore.

Not to say God doesn't forgive her, because He does. But we are the ones who have a problem with it. Sometimes we actually kick them out of our churches, by our actions! They already know they messed up, but *noooooo,* we have to rub it in their faces and make them feel even more like a failure. (The last time I checked, the Bible calls Satan an accuser [Zechariah 3:1]. Would you like to adopt that name as well? I hope not.)

OK. So what about kissing and stuff, Willy? Well, I know by my own experiences that kissing leads to grabbing, and grabbing leads to . . . *you know*! Some people say, "I have to test drive the car before I buy it!" Yeah, but that's the problem. You can't buy love! Your future spouse is a gift. Sex is a gift God gives you for free! So if God only gives you good gifts, according to the Bible, you think He's gonna give you a junky car, or a *hooptie*? No!

Ain't nothing better than when, on the day of your honeymoon, and you're both at the hotel, you tell your wife, "I don't know what to do!" And she tells you, "Me neither!" That's awesome. Now you guys can explore each other together. If you mess up, who cares. She doesn't know otherwise and vice versa.

I ain't gonna front, it was hard sometimes! At times my girlfriends would be like, "Don't come over tonight if we're not gonna do nothing." Other times I would say, "Baby, I gotta hang up the phone. *It's gettin' hot in here!*"

When I became a Christian, I vowed not to have sex ever again until the day of my marriage. I would pray like this: "Lord, take care of my future wife, whoever she might be." (So, even before meeting Lynette, I prayed for her for ten years!) I couldn't wait to give my future wife my all. There'd be times where I would fight with God: "Hurry up, Bro! I'm gonna blow!" But when I got converted, I made a pact with God that, with His help, I wouldn't have sex with another woman again that wasn't my wifey. And I didn't. Praise God.

You wanna know how Satan still got me? He got me through pornography. That was safe sex to me! I couldn't catch a disease or get anyone pregnant and dishonor God, but I was only fooling myself. I was dishonoring God big time. Wanna know why? The way I looked at women (His daughters) was changing. I was beginning to see them all as *fresh meat;* as instruments of sex, as hookers, if you will. And that is not right or normal and certainly not fair.

Not only that, I was still sinning. I was breaking multiple commandments, like wanting or coveting something or someone who wasn't mine. I was also killing; I was killing myself slowly—mentally, physically, financially, emotionally, and spiritually. The computer also became my god. I would spend more time on the computer late at night than with God when I did my devotion.

You see, that ain't good either! Somebody messed me up when I was little. I was introduced to porn by a cousin at the age of nine or ten! My mind, it's been messed up ever since. Yup, even until now.

Every once in a while I have a girl hit on me knowing I'm married, because Satan knows how to get me. The other day I was at the airport, and I spotted a famous wrestler. So I went up to her to see if I could take a picture to put on my Facebook page. I told her I was in town to preach, and she told me she was in town for a big Halloween party another wrestler was going to throw at a club; then, even after I told her I was a preacher, she said, "What time should my limo pick you up after you're done?"

What? Even as a married Christian man, that sounded very tempting—getting freaky with a celebrity! But you know what I did? I called my wife and immediately told her all about it. I disarmed the devil that way, or myself maybe. Pray for me, as I will pray for you.

I know it's hard—believe me, it is. It's still hard for me to take those images Satan has tattooed on my mind, the dirty pictures I've seen throughout my life. You know what I do now when I have the urge to turn on my computer when my wife is not home or is sleeping? I pray. I get on my knees and pray. You know what I do when Satan tells me, "Just do it"? Through prayer, I go to *Tools/Internet/Options,* then *Delete*! Believe me, I got it all down to a science! I disarm the devil.

My advice to you is to stop looking at images that are not getting you any closer to God. And pray as well. Pray that God will give you the strength to hold on until your wedding day. Pray for Him to help you stay away from porn, soft porn, YouTube, etc. In the meantime, I'll be home with my wife, unwrapping the *gift* He gave me (wink, wink).

---

1. Ellen G. White, *The Adventist Home,* 124.

Willy Ramos is an international evangelist, author, and co-author of several books, including *4GVN, 2 Catch a Thief, Changed,* and *Changed Too.* He's also a songwriter, recording artist, and movie director. He just finished writing, producing, and directing a short film entitled *SINtroduction* and is currently in pre-production on his next film. He lives in Orlando with his *gatita,* Lynette, and their son, Christian. His Web site is www.ghettopreacher.com.

CAN GOD'S SILENCE AWAKEN YOUR FAITH?

YAMILET BAZÁN

ASKING ME TO WRITE A CHAPTER ON LOSS IS like asking a stranger, "How did you get that scar?" When the person looks at the scar, immediately all of the memories of the event flood through his or her system, and you prepare yourself for a story. And sure enough, minutes later (sometimes hours), you emerge from this conversation with a new understanding and a new relationship with a totally random stranger.

Loss is a scar I keep hidden most of the time. Not so much because I don't want others to see it, but because I don't want to be reminded of it. There are moments when I don't feel like pretending, and so instead of putting on my strong face, I choose to let those nearby look deep inside my soul. And inevitably someone will begin to analyze and decide whether they will accept or reject my loss—my story. We can be good at that, can't we? As someone openly shares their brokenness, we quickly begin to fix it (with just the right dose of religious jargon), or we silently evaluate its merits. Just so you know, neither is helpful and neither leads to healing. Pain is rarely something that can be fixed.

What has surprised me most about loss is how quickly and suddenly, years after the event, all the same emotions and feelings can creep up on me, activated by the simplest little things. Maybe it will be an unexpected gesture such as a daughter grabbing hold of her mother's hand or an elderly couple sharing a gentle kiss. I can't explain when or why; I just know that all of a sudden I'm left breathless, with tears coming down my face and a resurfaced heart-wound that seems never to heal.

What happens when the fairy-tale story you imagined for yourself is suddenly shattered? When the God who could protect you from *anything*, the God of Shadrach, Meshach, and Abednego, does not show up in the fire and restore your situation? What happens when, like Joseph, you find yourself in a pit not of your making, and no matter how loud you scream, or how sincerely you reach out for God, His silence becomes unbearable? This is my story, recounting the day when the silence of God awakened my faith.

MY STORY

"But why, Lord?"

"Help me!"

"God?"

"What do I do?"

I sat on the cold tile floor, crunched up in a fetal position, hoping that the smaller I got, the smaller the pain could get too. I remember screaming, "I cannot take it anymore!" I forced myself to sit up and lean against the wall. Tears all gone, my body aching as if someone had physically beaten me up, my lungs struggling to inhale deeply, and my heart struggling to pump in rhythm. And then there was the silence. A silence so loud that it was almost eerie. I shook my head as if to help my mind accept how profoundly inadequate words seemed to be at this moment. I searched for hope in my memory bank . . . but finding none, I stared in silence.

We live in a world that has taught us "Just keep going" and "Don't worry, everything will be OK."

The church quickly joins in: "Have faith!"

"I can do everything with Christ!"

And for 95 percent of our lives, this works. But we will *all* encounter the moments (death of a loved one, relationships gone bad, parents' divorce, physical and sexual abuse by someone you trusted) when words fail, and you are left with a hole in your heart that cannot be filled. There is nothing that you can do to fill it.

Nothing. Ultimately my loss was not just a physical and emotional loss (it hardly ever is, right?). It was a loss of a well-crafted, religion-created God-ideal. God did not rescue me. He was not who I thought He was.

In other words, in Superman language, I encountered kryptonite and found myself powerless. No matter how hard I tried, it was as if all of my efforts left me pinned to the wall, with no answers, no Lois Lane, and Lex Luthor to contend with. Wasn't God going to intervene? Wouldn't He quickly remove my pain, "make all things right"? With God on my side, who can be against me? Our God is an awesome God . . . right?

You see, I thought for sure if I prayed hard enough, God could fix this situation. God could make it right. God could use me to change things. But when God did not fix it, I quickly shifted in my thinking: *God will take the pain away. He can fill this deep gaping hole if only I pray harder.* So imagine my surprise a year and a half later to find myself on the bathroom floor, empty and with an even deeper wound than when I began.

And then I heard myself begin to sing in the sobs, "I will praise You in the storm." I *will* praise You in the storm. I will praise *You* in the storm.

A miraculous moment of faith emerged through the pain. I sang those words for the next hour, giving my physical body permission to mourn the loss and reminding myself that just because I could not *see* Him and/or *feel* His presence, I would not stop recognizing the fact that He was there! "Though I walk through the valley of the shadow of death," David said, "I will fear no evil." "God is our refuge and strength, a very present help in trouble" (Psalm 23:4; 46:1, NKJV).

Yes, the pain of having to deal with an unforeseen reality was still very real. The pain of never being whole again and of having to endure those whispers, glances, and mean questions was still there. But something had changed. I had changed. I would never again be desperately seeking for God to "fix" or "fill" my wounded heart.

THAT WAS THEN, THIS IS NOW

I've come to realize that I had misinterpreted God's role in the human experience. From the beginning of the story of sin, we hear His sadness as He reveals to Adam and Eve that their life experience would be completely different from the one He had planned for them. Eating the forbidden fruit had broken the spiritual connection with the Creator, and our physical realm experienced the beginnings of a broken world.

Pain and suffering had entered planet Earth, and though God could not save the man and woman from the pain they were about to encounter, He went on to remind them that He would be there, and He would rewrite history. As a parent holds the hand of a child who has just fallen and scratched her knee, so God chose to walk through life with us and to hold our hand as we encounter Satan's most vicious attacks. Daily He whispers in our ear, "You are My beloved. I will never leave you nor forsake you."

Loss is humanity's companion. It was never in God's original plan, yet more than six thousand years later, there isn't a person alive who has not had to deal with its permanent scars. Through the years, I've spoken to survivors of many different types of loss. They all remind me that our living a God-filled life in the midst of a broken world is Satan's greatest defeat.

A NEW BEGINNING

I hope you realized as you read my story that this is really a hope story, not a loss story. In the end, like the crossing of the Red Sea for the people of Israel or the coming face to face with Goliath the giant for David, my experience awakened my sleeping faith. As Ellen White says, "Unbelief whispers, 'Let us wait till the obstructions are removed, and we can see our way clearly'; but faith courageously urges an advance, hoping all things, believing all things."[1]

My faith in the unseen and very present God

emerged and began to create a new road for me to travel. I now walk in faith. I choose daily to live joyfully in His presence, remembering His creation story is still being lived out in me. My scar still hurts. Yet it does not define me, but rather it serves to remind me of the day I "praised Him in the storm," and He, in turn, taught me to believe. I share my scar in hopes that you, too, can someday be able to look at yours and find in it hope and healing.

---

1. Ellen G. White, *Patriarchs and Prophets* (Mountain View, Calif.: Pacific Press®, 1958), 290.

Yamilet Bazán, BA, MA, and soon-to-be graduate of Andrews University (PhD), Yami has been involved in education and youth ministries for the past seventeen years. She cares deeply for young people and has dedicated her life to serving God, youth, and her beloved Adventist church. She began as an educator, continued as a minister, served as Associate Youth Director of her conference for eight years, and now is the Vice President at La Sierra University. Her passion is to set the record straight about God and the truth we hold so dear. She's been married for nineteen years and has a son named Daniel.

AT THE MERCY OF DADDY

Carlos A. Camacho

H E ABUSED ME, PASTOR." THOSE WERE THE last words she said to me before she started to cry. The victim had been a beautiful blue-eyed, blond girl, not more than eight years old, and now she was an adult. The perpetrator: her own father. Married and divorced twice, this woman was on the verge of losing her third marriage. She was a beautiful person with far-away, grown-up children who didn't know her well and didn't want to. She sat in the pew just about every week with a pleasant smile and a heavy heart.

As an eight-year-old girl, she was the victim of a father's perverted mind. She had run away and married the first man she could find, just to get away from home, and had always managed to get into abusive relationships. As an adult, she ended up back at home, only to be reminded how much mental, physical, and emotional power Dad had over her.

I cried many times in the hours I shared with her as I remembered my own pain and brokenness. I met her father a few months later, a very old, heavy-set man, on his deathbed. I could not avoid a feeling of release in knowing he was not going to be able to destroy any more lives.

I asked "Why?" many times, but there was never a voice from heaven or a light from up above to enlighten me, only sadness and confusion. A person who has been abused feels real emotional pain, feelings that shouldn't have been awakened—sadness, depression, fear, hatred, and guilt. The feelings seem to take over every aspect of one's life. Children shouldn't have to deal with abuse, especially at the hands of the one person who's supposed to protect them and instill in them a sense of value and security. Sometimes you find yourself wondering, *Does anyone really care?*

DOES ANYBODY REALLY CARE?

Early in my ministry, before I became a full-time pastor, I had to endure the pain and despair of someone close to my heart, a new church member. This young single mother asked to talk to me. She opened up her heart and poured out to me her pain and hatred. She had just learned that her little daughter was being molested by someone close to them—someone she trusted, someone she considered family, as is often the case.

We talked, cried, prayed, and after much discussion, attempted to put the past behind and move on. Believe me, when there's been abuse, trying to move on and put the past behind you is not that simple and oftentimes impossible. Sin is very messy. The sin of one person affects many people deeply.

Years have gone by, and the little daughter is now a beautiful young woman. We talk sometimes. She struggles constantly. She often wonders if anybody really cares for her; she wonders why her father doesn't seem to make an effort to be in touch with her. She often feels abandoned. She's been kicked out of her house on more than one occasion and is now trying to deal with the emotional pain and guilt of an abortion. She has wondered, time after time, why she doesn't seem to keep emotionally steady, and I'm afraid there's never been a good answer.

Maybe you are in the same boat as I am sometimes, thinking, *It's not Jesus I'm afraid of, but some of His followers.*

Well into my ministry, I was working for a popular evangelist doing a citywide crusade to bring the good news of the gospel to people. It was my job to take care of the visitors. We contacted them, gave them Bible studies, and helped them make their decisions for

Christ. Toward the end of the evangelistic effort, on the night before the last sermon, I went to visit someone I'll call "Lovely." I was hoping she would be interested in baptism. I made my speech and extended an invitation. She assured me she loved the Lord and that she really liked the church, but she wasn't going to be baptized. I pushed her on it, she refused, so I backed off. I thanked Lovely for her time and left her home.

The next morning, I was scheduled to be the translator for the last sermon. Lovely came in and asked to talk to me. I asked my friend to help with the work so I could speak to Lovely. I could sense the seriousness of her request just by looking at her face.

We stepped out of the convention center and, sitting on a bench across from a beautiful fountain, I heard one of the saddest stories I've ever heard about my own people and my own church, the church I love dearly.

Lovely had worked as a live-in maid when she was a young woman, in the home of Seventh-day Adventist family. This had happened many years earlier in her country of origin. As it turned out, she had known about the church ever since she was young. And boy, she knew a lot about the church! The man of the household held a position at the local church. She quickly became familiar with the church as she lived with this family.

She remembered liking church, and soon she felt the calling to be baptized, but there was one problem she felt she needed to solve. The man had forced himself on her, and she had become his lover. She was an inexperienced young girl who had never been to the city before.

In her desperation and confusion, she went to another church official to ask for help. She told me, "I'm not sure exactly what happened, but I got kicked out of the house, I got kicked out of the church, and they told me not to ever come back." She was left completely alone in a big city she didn't know, without a job or a place to sleep, feeling used and abused, and feeling overwhelming guilt.

After finishing her story, she said simply, "I love God and I can feel Him calling me into baptism, but I'm afraid of *you guys*." I did not see that one coming. I cried with her. I asked for forgiveness on behalf of my church, and all I could say time after time was, "I'm sorry. I understand now."

I continued to work with Lovely and had the awesome privilege of baptizing her and her daughter a few months later. She had lived most of her life thinking religion and God were a fraud. She had endured the suffering of feeling rejected by people and, as a consequence, by God, and many times she had to fight suicidal thoughts. When I think about her, all I can say is, shame on us; shame on me as a pastor when I don't work to make sure my church is a safe place; shame on me when I pretend everything is all right and close my eyes to reality.

NO ONE DESERVES TO BE ABUSED

There is a basic principle: No human being should suffer at the hands of another human being. That is a direct violation of God's desire for us. God has not called us to anything less than being kind to one another. Abuse at any level is wrong. Whether physical, sexual, psychological, or religious, abuse does not fit into the plan of God for our lives.

The question follows: How do you deal with the pain of abuse? How do you deal with unresolved issues of the past? How do you deal with things that are happening to you in the present? I'm going to give you some general ideas because I recognize that each case is unique.

Abuse is illegal. If you are under eighteen, there are many laws to protect you and many ways to bring healing to your heart. You need to speak up. You need to report abuse. If abuse is happening, you need, by all means, to stop the abuse right now! You don't deserve it, and it is not your fault. You must have a lot of questions, and I'm pretty sure you're afraid.

Think about this: think about your life free of resentment, guilt, and fear—and go for it. Stop the abuse now and begin a process of healing and restoration. Go see someone and begin a new life with Christ. It is possible. I am living proof. I have witnessed restoration many times.

If you are in an abusive relationship right now, you don't have to be. He or she is not going to change and get better unless that individual recognizes the sin, deals with it, and finds professional help. If you're dating an abusive boyfriend or girlfriend, you need to get out of that relationship. If you're married, seek counsel right now, and resolve to do something about it, whether you end up divorced or not.

If you're dealing with anger issues and have become a perpetrator yourself, if you sometimes "lose it" and feel the need to take it out on someone close, *seek help*! It's not normal. You shouldn't have to deal with that, so find help. Find help before you hurt someone or end up in jail. God loves you too much for you not to seek help. If you have some kind of addiction and attraction toward children or teenagers, *seek help*. Praying is good, but please, please, please, *find professional help*. There are people who can help you. Really help you.

If you are in an abusive relationship and find yourself fearing for your life, be very careful. The primary suspect in a murder case is always the spouse or the boyfriend or girlfriend. Be smart. Look at the signs, open your eyes, be honest with yourself, and come up with an escape plan. Put some money away, have an extra set of car and house keys, talk to a friend who can come get you at any time. Keep a cell phone handy. The best thing to do is to simply leave before you have to escape.

Every story is different, and each one comes with its own complications. We often think we're the only ones going through a situation, but we are not, unfortunately. Abuse is so complex and so much a taboo subject that there's not a perfect, "one size fits all" solution. In all cases, victims of abuse have to work hard to get well.

The good news is, there is help! Please don't put off getting help by excuses like "I don't have money," "I'm not *that* bad off," "I'm much better now." If you're dealing with pain, shame, fear, and guilt, to name a few emotions, you need professional help. Pastors are good as an initial contact who might be able to provide a referral, but seek professional help. Look for someone who values both scientifically proven methods and techniques and God as the center of all genuine healing.

WE CAN OVERCOME

When I was a kid, someone close to the family, a

young adult, tried to convince me to "play" with each other's genitals. Even at a young age, I suspected that wasn't normal. He even tried to touch me while I was asleep. I woke up and ran away. I wasn't able to sleep after that. I remember feeling very guilty and afraid, and I had a lot of hatred in my heart. I felt robbed, and those "little incidents," which could have been far worse, affected me the rest of my childhood and adolescence. It literally felt as though something broke inside of me. I didn't talk about it for years and kept it all in. I just didn't know what to do. I had issues with trusting God and developed an addictive personality; I would take showers for hours because I felt dirty.

Now, here's the thing: I'm not going to sit here and tell you that I'm doing really well now or that there are no issues anymore. I can't tell you that because those two incidents and other issues of my childhood tried to steal away the love of God from my heart. I used to think that the ultimate quest for Christians was to find happiness as if it were hiding somewhere and all you had to do was look really hard till you found it. But life has showed me otherwise.

As real as God's promise of the final prize—salvation— may be, He has also said we would have to go through difficulties on our way to heaven. The other thing He's promised is this: "I'm going to be with you every step of the way!" Can you see that? No matter what your situation is, God loves you passionately, and He's promised you both salvation and protection as you face trials and temptation. You need to know it, understand it, and write it on the walls of your heart.

My years of high school were crucial years. I became aware of my pain and confronted my demons. I did it through conversations with teachers and friends and many sessions of prayer. Also, I did lots of reading of what I call the "healing duo": *Steps to Christ* and *The Desire of Ages,* by Ellen G. White, along with other, more technical books. Education doesn't bring you healing, but it does bring you awareness. Through all those things, I began my healing process. Later, as an adult, I looked for professional help on three different occasions.

One of the ways God has brought both healing and assurance to my life is by bringing people into my life and ministry who are looking for help. I used to wonder why, but not anymore. As my good friend Willy says, "Your mess can become your message!" God has turned the work of the enemy into a big blessing for others, and I feel grateful to know that God can change you and me in spite of the circumstances of our lives.

THE HIDDEN FILES OF YOUR SUBCONSCIOUS

"How are you doing?" I asked a young girl once.

With a big sigh, she said, "Not good!"

The question prompted many discussions and ended at the office of a professional counselor. On the outside she seemed normal, bright, and full of life, a girl whose life seemed to have been planned carefully by some higher power. But on the inside she was dying. She fought depression, eating disorders, suicidal thoughts, shame, guilt, and low self-esteem. Because she was a Christian and her family was held in high regard in the church, she thought she simply needed to pray harder and just grow out of her misery.

She could vaguely remember but wasn't sure about the details of an incident that took place when she was a child. She remembered her uncle doing something inappropriate that made her feel terrible. She couldn't remember it very well, and she tried to avoid thinking about it. On the other hand, she couldn't figure out why she felt as bad she did, when she had everything a young teenager needed.

Our bodies are complex, and God made us in such a perfect way that when we go through physical trauma, our minds have a way to shut off, and we faint or lose consciousness. Our emotional system works in a similar way; our emotions can shut down, and when we experience great emotional pain and our young, undeveloped minds are not able to process and understand, our emotions file those experiences in "hidden files." The experiences show up again later in many ways and forms, telling us that we can't achieve true happiness and peace and reminding us constantly that something is wrong with us. That's why we need professional help. God has equipped professionals with tools that can help you. I stand boldly before you to assure you that there is help and that you can find it.

God has been with you along the way. God knows your pain and shame. God knows you, and He's suffered with you every step of the way. There's not one tear you've cried that God hasn't seen or cried with you. He loves you. He paid a high price for you through His Son, Jesus Christ, and He is not going to leave you to chance. He's waiting for you to come and seek Him and seek help. God made you for joy and happiness, and even in this messed-up world we're living in, God longs to give you peace and love.

BEAUTY FOR ASHES

Jesus talked about His own mission here on earth, citing Isaiah 61:3. He said He had come "to care for the needs of all who mourn in Zion, give them bouquets of roses instead of ashes, messages of joy instead of news of doom, a praising heart instead of a languid spirit. Rename them 'Oaks of Righteousness' planted by God to display his glory" (*The Message*). Other Bible versions say, "I'll give you beauty for ashes." Whichever way you want to read it, God has promised to restore your soul and your emotions. Please do not let the evil one tell you otherwise.

Sometimes you may wonder, *If God is God, and if He's as powerful as people say He is, and if He loves us as He says He does, why does He let us hurt so much?* I'm going to be honest and tell you there's no easy answer, especially when you're dealing with an aching heart. But out of my own experience I can assure you that even though the evil one claimed power and authority over this world, and the world has been declining since that time, God has always been present, and He has always been a refuge to those who let Him come into their lives.

Let me invite you to ask a different question. Don't ask Why? because you may never find an answer; instead, ask *How?* How can I overcome? How can I find help? How can I feel better? How can I move beyond me, so I can help those around me? God will speak to you and guide you to find healing and peace if you will only let Him.

Would you pray this prayer with me? "Lord, thank You for loving me the way You do. Thank You for Your sacrifice on the cross of Calvary. You know me and the things that I've gone through since I was a tiny baby. I need healing, and I know You can heal me. Please guide me through the right steps on my way to feeling peace and happiness even in the midst of difficulties. Thank You, Jesus. Amen."

It turns out, we're all at the mercy of Daddy. Not an earthly daddy but a heavenly Daddy. His love and mercy are with you always. He'll heal the wounds of your heart and embrace you throughout eternity. You are under the mercy of Abba Father, that is, God, your Daddy!

SWEETNESS
FOR YOUR
BITTERNESS

CARLOS ACOSTA

I WAS SITTING AT A TABLE WITH A YOUNG WOMAN, talking with her about her problems. She told me that it was hard for her to live a fulfilling life and to experience wholeness. However, I knew something else was bothering her. As we continued, she opened up and shared her battle with the past. Two years earlier, she had been physically abused by a relative she had trusted, and she could not see herself moving on from that experience. She was having difficulty even falling sleep at night because of the memories of this horrible encounter. I shared with her God's way of dealing with those who have hurt us: forgiveness.

Many young people today face the challenge of dealing appropriately with those who have hurt them. Some have been abused, neglected, abandoned, rejected, attacked, or taken advantage of—and they don't know how to overcome their resentment and suffering. You might be struggling with this experience, and though you consider yourself to be a good, kind, and loving person, you harbor a grudge against someone, and you plan on keeping it that way and have even thought about getting revenge. You think that the person does not deserve to be forgiven either by you or by God.

If that is how you feel, I am hoping and praying that this could be the time when everything changes for you. I am praying that God can help you make choices that lead you to forgive the unforgivable. And if you have not been hurt deeply, I pray that you will use these words to help someone else who is struggling because he or she is unable or unwilling to forgive.

WHAT FORGIVENESS IS NOT

The predominant concept of forgiveness comes from the Jewish teaching, spread by the rabbis, which said that you must forgive only someone who was remorseful and had asked to be forgiven. In other words, you just don't forgive spontaneously; you wait on the other person to see if he or she wants to be forgiven. However, as we will see, this is not the true biblical concept of forgiveness. For now, let us clarify what forgiveness is not.

Forgiveness is not *justifying, understanding,* or *explaining why the person acted toward you as he or she did.* We shouldn't try to understand the evil that was done to us because in doing that, we will create an excuse that doesn't exist. For example, if you say that someone physically abused you because you were wearing something too provocative or because you were walking down the street late at night or because you accepted the invitation to enter his or her house without others present, that would be putting the blame on you instead of on the person who committed the atrocity. So, don't try to justify, understand, or explain the evil that was done to you.

Also, forgiveness is not *forgetting about the offense and trusting time to take care of it.* Believe me, a lot of people remember precisely how, when, and who hurt them, even if they have forgiven them. Scars from painful experiences are not forgotten. The fact that you remember shows that it was real and significant. So, don't buy into the idea of "forgive and forget" because forgetting is impossible. God is the only One who can "forgive and forget."[1] You and I will remember what was done to us. Why is that? Through pain, we can learn about life and we can grow, and that is why we remember. God doesn't need such reminders.

Last, forgiveness is not *denying that you were hurt just because there are others who have suffered more.* Your pain is real, and you should not dismiss it or lessen it by comparing it to the pain of others. Yes, there might be people who have suffered worse things than you have, but that doesn't make your pain less real or meaning-ful. Don't reject the truthfulness of your pain. Regard-less of how big or small it might seem to be, if it affects you, then it has to be dealt with.

WHAT FORGIVENESS IS ALL ABOUT

We mentioned earlier the Jewish teaching that says that for you to forgive someone, that person must show remorse and that he or she must ask for forgiveness be-fore you grant it. However, when we look at Jesus, we find that He did not follow that mistaken concept. Pe-ter, one of Jesus' disciples, asked Him, "Lord, how many times shall I forgive my brother or sister who sins against me? Up to seven times?" (Matthew 18:21, NIV). We have to keep in mind that when Peter said, "up to seven times," he was showing off. Jewish teach-ing said that a person was bound to forgive someone only three times, so by saying "seven times," Peter was trying to look good before his Master.

However, Jesus answered, "I tell you, not seven times, but seventy-seven times" (verse 22, NIV). With this statement, Jesus tears down the false concept of conditional forgiveness and brings forgiveness into a new light. He taught that forgiveness doesn't have a limit, and it doesn't have any prerequisites for you to exercise it. Jesus said that if someone has something against you, you should go and forgive that person (see Matthew 5:23, 24). In other words, forgiveness is not dependent on what the other person does, but it is a decision we make on our own, even if the other person doesn't want forgiveness. It is about what you do and not about the other person.

Let's take a closer look at this truth. First of all, forgiveness benefits you more than the other person. You are the recipient of the blessing that comes from forgiving. The moment you choose to forgive, it will allow you to begin to heal and will lead you into a peaceful and wholesome experience. In a sense, forgiveness is a self-serving act because, by exercising it, you will be the biggest beneficiary. You will not be forgiving for the sake of the other person but for your own.

Let me give you an illustration from the world of accounting. Let's say you borrow a significant amount of money from a bank. You run into difficulties and are not able to pay that loan back. After filing a few lawsuits against you and trying any way it can to recover the capital, the bank realizes you are not able to pay the money back, and so it decides to take a different route. After giving your name to all the credit agencies so that you won't get any loans in the future, the bank decides to forgive your debt. You are ecstatic and joyful.

However, this doesn't mean that you could go into the bank the next day and say, "Thank you for forgiving my debt, and by the way, can I get another loan?" They will kick you out in no time! Why? Because what they forgave was not for your sake but theirs. Even though some might say that you are getting the benefit of this action, in reality a bank will forgive a debt for its own good. This is a way of cutting losses, moving on, and being able to deal with other responsibilities. It's a selfish act that benefits the one who extends the forgiveness.

Similarly, Jesus reminds us that when we forgive, we will reap the benefits of this action. When you forgive, it is as if you are saying, "Those people don't owe me anything anymore, because they are bankrupt. They can't pay me, so I'm canceling this debt so that I can move on." I can do this because I understand that God has forgiven me even more, and out of gratitude for what God has done in my life, I will grant them forgiveness.

Colossians 2:13, 14 may be the best explanation of what forgiveness is about. The apostle Paul says that God forgave our debt. What debt? Our sins. How did God do this? He gave His Son. What does that mean? God canceled the debt of our sins and nailed it to the cross of Jesus, and because of this, we can enjoy the hope of salvation and the reality of forgiveness from our sins. In the same manner, when you forgive, you are canceling a debt that someone else owes you, and you arc deciding to move on.

FORGIVENESS VERSUS RECONCILIATION

Some have confused forgiveness with reconciliation. Forgiveness is a decision in which the other person doesn't take part, while reconciliation has to do with both people partaking in the process of coming together. It's important that we understand this difference. Jesus said over and over that we should forgive those who have hurt us (Matthew 6:14, 15; Luke 6:36, 37; Ephesians 4:32). However, He didn't say that when we forgive, everything will be fixed so that it's the same as before. Sometimes this reconciliation happens, but other times it doesn't.

The story of Irma will help me illustrate this. As a single mom, she had experienced physical, emotional, and sexual abuse by her partner. This man inflicted a lot of pain and made her life miserable. One day, after she had been brutally beaten, Irma had had enough and decided to walk away with her two kids. She didn't have any money and ended up in a relative's home. They happened to be Christians and took her to church. I had a chance to talk to Irma many times about forgiveness, but she struggled with the thought of forgiving her partner because she thought that if she forgave him, she'd have to go back to him.

Like many others, she had confused forgiveness with reconciliation. God helped her understand the difference, and she felt joy and peace once she decided to forgive, realizing that she could go on with her life without this man. You can ask God to give you the courage to forgive, and if there can be reconciliation, great. But if there can't be, that's OK also.

WHAT ABOUT REVENGE?

Don't we say that revenge is sweet? Some people defend the idea of revenge as the best way to deal with those who have wounded you. However, let me ask you to think about these questions: First, how far are you willing to take your revenge? I mean, if you do something to hurt that person, what would happen if he or she also decides to take revenge on you? When would it ever stop? Friends, there are a lot of stories of young people who got even with those who hurt them, only to suffer even more as they are filled with more anger in their hearts. We have others who have sought revenge and are now in a wheelchair, in jail, or even worse, dead. Revenge is only for God. Don't try to take His job.

The Bible tells us, "Do not take revenge, my dear friends, but leave room for God's wrath, for it is written: 'It is mine to avenge; I will repay,' says the Lord" (Romans 12:19, NIV). He knows how and when to deal with those who have done wrong to you. He is infinitely more informed, wise, and just than you can ever be. In His time, He will take care of those who have hurt you. If you want an example of this truth, just look at O. J. Simpson. Sooner or later, you get what you deserve.

WHAT IF I JUST DON'T WANT TO FORGIVE?

People who refuse to forgive hurt themselves. They can't sleep. Ulcers line their stomachs. Their blood pressure rises. They see the negative in every situation because their lives are polluted with feelings of resentment and anger. People who are unwilling to forgive may feel that they are punishing the other person, but they are the only person paying the price.[2]

Try a simple experiment on yourself. Make a fist and hold it tight. One minute of this is sufficient to bring discomfort. Consider what would happen if you kept that fist in a state of tension during a period that extended into weeks, months, or even years. Obviously, it would soon become a sick member of the body.

Perhaps the wound is old. A parent abused you. A

teacher slighted you. And you are angry. Perhaps the wound is fresh. The friend who owes you money just drove by in a new car. The boss who hired you with promises of promotions has forgotten how to pronounce your name. Your circle of friends went on a weekend getaway, and you weren't invited. And you are hurt.[3]

Part of you is broken, and the other part is bitter. Part of you wants to cry, and part of you wants to fight. The tears you cry are hot because they come from your heart, where a fire is burning. It's the fire of anger. It is blazing, it is consuming you, and you are left with a decision to make: Do I put the fire out or heat it up? Do I get over it or get even? Do I release it or resent it? Do I let my hurts heal, or do I let hurt turn into hate? Resentment is the deliberate decision to nurse the offense until it becomes a black, furry, growling grudge.[4]

Unfaithfulness is wrong. Revenge is bad. But the worst part of all is that, without forgiveness, bitterness is all that's left. When you forgive, you are not letting the other person off the hook, but rather you are freeing yourself from the bondage of that pain. There is no other way to find healing from your past wounds than to forgive.

FORGIVENESS, GOD'S STYLE

The Bible tells us, "God put the world square with himself through the Messiah, giving the world a fresh start by offering the forgiveness of sins. . . . How, you say? In Christ. God put on him the wrong who never did anything wrong, so you could be put right with God" (2 Corinthians 5:19–21, *The Message*). It reminds us that we have been forgiven of our debt. Jesus took it upon Himself to pay for our sins so that you can assume His fortune, which is forgiveness.

Because of what God has done for us, He asks us to forgive. If you are grateful for God's forgiveness, then forgive others. Think about the many mistakes and sins you have committed. The list may be so long that you can't even comprehend it. However, God reminds you that regardless of how long, how bad, how ugly, how deep your sins might be, He is willing to forgive you if you only ask. No strings are attached. His forgiveness is there for the taking. It will bring hope and a new start to your life. Don't forget: you will never forgive anyone more than God has already forgiven you.

PRACTICAL ADVICE

Remember the story of Joseph in Genesis 45:1–15? Take a look at it right now. And then let me point out some general guidelines that will help you as you begin to forgive those who have hurt you:

Take your time. If it takes you a while to forgive, that's OK. It took Joseph years to see his brothers again, and I believe this was necessary to get him ready to forgive. True forgiveness takes time, so don't rush into it. Pray and ask God to help you do it.

Take the initiative. Don't wait for anyone else to do this for you. Take charge. This means that if you have to write a letter, make a phone call, or talk face to face with that other person to express what you feel, go ahead.

Talk specifically about the problem. Don't assume the other person knows what you're talking about. Be specific about what it is that you're forgiving. Don't just say, "You hurt me and I forgive you." Tell exactly what happened.

Express your feelings. Don't excuse it, don't dismiss it, but be honest and deal with the pain. Guided by the Spirit of God, this can be a turning point for you. As you express what you feel, conclude by saying that because God has forgiven you, you have also decided to forgive.

After doing this, live knowing that the pain the other person caused you is no longer with you because you have deposited it in the hands of God. You will continue to remember what happened, but you will remember even more how God led you to forgive and how He has helped you to heal.

The young woman I spoke about at the beginning

of this chapter listened as I told her about the beauty of forgiveness. After a few months I was able to visit with her again, and she told me that she had decided to forgive and was now experiencing the healing touch of God. She said, "I still remember what he did to me, but I can say with gratitude in my heart that the pain has dwindled and the scars remind me of the healing God has allowed me to experience because I decided to forgive." Remember, "Forgiveness is giving up the possibility of a better past and the raising of a limitless future." Try it, and you won't regret it.

1. Dave Stoops, "New Life Live: October 14, 2011," *New Life Live With Steve Arterburn,* podcast audio, October 14, 2011, http://newlife.com/new-life-live -october-14-2011/.

2. Max Lucado, *Let the Journey Begin: God's Roadmap for New Beginnings* (Nashville: Thomas Nelson, 2009), 71.

3. Robert W. Harvey and David G. Benner, *Understanding and Facilitating Forgiveness: A Short-Term Structured Model* (Grand Rapids, Mich.: Baker Books, 1996), 59.

4. Max Lucado, *Let the Journey Begin,* 71.

CHILD OF GOD
CITIZEN OF THE WORLD
AND HEAVEN

JOSÉ CORTÉS

JUST THE OTHER DAY I SAT DOWN WITH MY TWO sons, my six-year-old, José III, and my four-year-old, Joel Benjamin. They were asking some simple questions. "Where are we from? What are we [referring to nationality]? Why do we speak Spanish?" I explained to them that I had been born in Cuba, and their mom, my wife, Joanne, was born in Australia, the daughter of an Irish-Australian father and a Chilean mother.

I thought I had at least answered one of their questions, yet as I finished my explanation, they asked, "So what are we? Are we Cuban or Australian?"

Trying to find out what was on their minds, I asked them, "What would you like to be?"

My little boy Joel said, "I am from Cuba."

But José, my older son, said, "Papá, I was born in New York. I am a New Yorker." And looking at an American flag across the street in our neighbor's yard, he added, "And that flag is our flag, right, Papá?"

Having heard his older brother, Joel had a quick comeback and said, "Well, I am a New Yorker, Cuban, and Australian, and that is my flag too."

Finally, José, who likes to excel in his conversations, trying to outdo his brother, came back and said, "I am an American, New Yorker, Cuban, Australian, and a little bit Chilean too, Papá. I am almost from the whole world, and I belong to Jesus, so I am from heaven too."

José III had it totally right. As people living on this planet, we must cherish our roots, value our heritage, and build on our background. If we want to live the life that God wants us to live and experience our fullest potential, we must be citizens of the world, with appreciation and love for all people everywhere on this globe. Of course, we never forget that someone who believes in Jesus should be a great citizen of this world but also a citizen of God's kingdom, with access to eternal life and all its privileges.

The Bible says, "You are no longer strangers and foreigners, but fellow citizens with the saints and members of the household of God" (Ephesians 2:19, NKJV).

NEVER FORGET WHERE YOU CAME FROM

Though your identity is not defined by your heritage, it is important that you never forget where you came from. Your place of birth, your parents, your culture, your race, your age, and your gender are important factors in your life, which you must celebrate and use to build on.

I will never forget where I came from. I was born in the city of Pinar del Rio, Cuba. The name for those born in that city is "Pinareños." If you Google that word, you will see that most of the results will be links to jokes about the citizens of Pinar del Rio.

One of the most famous jokes about Pinareños is about a time they were building a theater in Pinar del Rio and the builders left the cement mixer inside the building. When the building was finished, they could not get the cement mixer out of the building, so they had to break a wall, get the equipment out, and then build the wall again. I've heard people say that it is a true story. If you go online, that's one of the things my hometown is famous for. And there are plenty of other jokes.

When my mother was six months pregnant with me, my dad, an Adventist pastor in Pinar del Rio, was put in prison by the Communist government of Cuba, which had made it a priority to mistreat and persecute some religious leaders. I was born while he was in prison. The first time my father came to see me, he was escorted by guards and handcuffed as if he were a criminal. We are grateful to God that he was freed days after my birth.

When we left Cuba, my family moved to Madrid, Spain. We had to leave all of our belongings and were able to take only four suitcases. We took our best clothes, but our best Cuban clothes did not look very good in Madrid. The Communist Cuba fashion is not fashionable in Europe. As soon as we got off the plane, we and everybody else knew we were foreigners.

The loving people of the church in Madrid took us to the Dorcas Society room that was filled with nice clothes donated by people in the church and community for the needy. I remember how excited my brother and I were as we were given many nice shirts, pants, coats, and shoes that Monday afternoon.

On Sabbath we came to church, and of course, we were all wearing the clothes we had received from the Dorcas room. I was really excited about my new clothes till a kid in the church told me that my dad was wearing a suit that had belonged to his now deceased grandfather and my sweater used to belong to his brother, who had outgrown it. Those were humbling and difficult moments for a teenager like me.

Later we moved to the United States. My first day in eleventh grade at the Rancocas Regional High School in Mount Holly, New Jersey, was very interesting. My name was not on the chemistry teacher's roster. When Mr. Sullivan did roll call, he did not call my name. He approached me and extended his hand, asking me to show him my class schedule. I did not understand his question, and since I saw his hand extended toward me, I shook his hand and said, "Fine, thank you." The whole class laughed. I spoke very little English.

I could tell you many more stories, but please get my point. Your background and life experiences can bring you down and bury you. But it does not have to be that way; with the help of God, they can serve as motivators to move you forward. Your past does not have to predict your future, and your determination and your trust in the blessings of God can outdo any disadvantages you were born in or grew up with. Look around you. Most people who make it big in life had to deal with disadvantage and negative experiences. The Bible is full of those stories too. Joseph was a foreign prisoner and became the governor of Egypt. Ruth was a foreign widow and became the grandmother of King David. Esther was a foreign orphan and became queen of the Persians.

Let your heritage, whether good or bad, positive or negative, privileged or disadvantaged, serve as a launching pad in the hands of God. If you forget where you came from, you will not be able to give God thanks for the awesome things He has done in your life. Today my father is the president of the Adventist Church in New Jersey, my mother is an auditor for the church, my little brother is a pediatrician in Florida, and I serve God as the director of Adventist youth ministries for the Seventh-day Adventist Church in the North Atlantic region of the United States and the country of Bermuda. I am not saying this to boast, but to make it clear that God is able to take a kid from a city that could not handle a cement mixer, a kid who could not speak a word of English in high school, and use him for His glory.

If you are growing up in a poor home, it does not mean that you always have to be poor. If your brother is doing drugs, drinks a lot, and is involved with gangs, you don't have to do what he does. If your dad abuses your mom, and your home is broken, you can still have a beautiful family of your own one day. Your past does not determine your future. Your determination, your choices, and the blessings of God will lift you up to a different level and move you forward. But when you get there, don't forget where you came from.

A CITIZEN OF THE WORLD

In my thirty-nine years of life, I have lived through some very interesting moments. I remember one time when someone told me, "You are qualified for this ministry post, but we are looking for an Anglo." I once heard, "We know you could have done a great job, but this time it is an African American's turn." Years ago I was also told, "The reason why you got the job is that they were looking for a Hispanic." I have seen women who have been denied an opportunity because of their gender. Several times I have heard, "You are too young." To be fair, I must say that I have also heard the younger generation reject perfectly qualified individuals because they think of them as too old.

At times it seems that a big part of life is racism, nationalism, chauvinism, tribalism, and generational wars. I have seen people within their ethnic groups reject others because they come from a different country. I have seen others suggest that people from their country are the best simply because they are from their country.

Let's be clear and put some things in perspective here: all races, generations, nationalities, and both genders have great people whom you can be proud of and, equally, people whom you would be ashamed of. Your ethnicity, nationality, gender, and age are a very important part of your life, but they definitely do not define your worth.

Your value is defined by the fact that you are a child of God. The decisions you make, your attitude, your common sense, your preparation, and your competence are bonuses. They do not add human value but are helpful as you find your place in the community, the workplace, and the church, and you excel the way God wants you to.

As you find your identity in this world, keep in mind that no one is more valuable than you are. By the same token, you are not more valuable than anyone else. Our worth is equal before God. When the good old boys try to patronize you because of your age, don't feel bitter or take it personally. Pray for them that God will help them to learn and to be more concerned about the cause than about themselves. When someone misjudges you because of your ethnicity (either that you are in the majority or the minority—prejudice goes in both directions), don't feel like a second-class citizen, but ask God to take away the prejudice.

When someone denies you because of your gender, don't feel sorry for yourself. Feel bad for those who ignore that God also has a plan for your life, and pray that God will take away the ignorance. Don't let the assumptions or lack of knowledge of others dictate who you are. You are who you are because God created you in His image and because of the decisions that you make with your life.

Don't let politicians or others in the public arena

take you for granted. There are some who believe that because you are rich or look a certain way, you will always vote for them; others claim that because you are poor and from certain ethnic groups, you owe them a vote. Don't let anyone take you for granted, but support competence, integrity, and good results above race, language, age, or political affiliation.

I have seen people who are so identified with a political cause that they would vote for the devil, even if it kills them, just to be loyal to their interest group. It is my personal belief that a child of God who wants to maximize his or her potential in the twenty-first century should be a citizen of the world, one who loves and respects all people regardless of their color, language, gender, or age.

Don't get caught in prejudice, gender, or generational wars. Don't wait for others to change in order to make your move, but begin to change this world with the man in the mirror, the woman in the mirror. If you don't begin the change, the world, your community, and the church will never be a better place.

A CHILD OF GOD

A lot has changed in my life since the day I was born in Pinar del Rio, Cuba, and my dad visited me from the prison, escorted by the Communist guards. It's been many years since I was told that I was wearing the outgrown sweater of another teen in Madrid. Though English continues to be my second language, I now understand enough not to shake a teacher's hand when he asks for my class schedule. Yet there is one thing that has not changed through all these years: the fact that I am a child of God. That's my identity; that is who I am. Above being a citizen of the world, I am a citizen of God's kingdom.

While in this world, celebrate and cherish your heritage and build on your background. After all, there is nothing that you can do about who your parents are, your birthplace, the color of your skin, your height, or your age. However, you can choose your attitude every day. You can study hard day in and day out, you can choose your work ethic, and you can be a law-abiding citizen. Above all things, there is one issue you do have a say on: where you will spend eternity. Though you could not help your beginning, you can choose your ultimate future, and it can be awesome. Eternity with Jesus!

You are a child of God, which makes you royalty, so don't be surprised if, next time I see you, I call you "Your Highness!"

LA COSA NOSTRA

WILLY RAMOS

> "Teacher," said John, "we saw someone driving out demons in Your name and we told him to stop, because he was not one of us."
>
> "Do not stop him," Jesus said. ". . . For whoever is not against us is for us" (Mark 9:38–40, NIV).

I SAW A MAN GET KILLED RIGHT IN FRONT OF ME LIKE ten years ago, before I became a Christian. His younger brother, a Mafia kingpin, gave orders to one of his henchmen to shoot the guy as he fished, while he stood there and watched emotionless from his lake house.

Sound familiar? Isn't that a Hollywood movie? Does that kind of stuff happen in real life? The answer to both of those questions is Yes. The movie was *The Godfather: Part II*. (And, yes, I did see it in front of me, but on a TV screen after renting it from Blockbuster while eating some Little Debbie snacks! You know how I do!)

Al Pacino's character, Michael Corleone, approved the hit on his older brother, Fredo, after Fredo tried to have him killed because they passed him over and the family business went to Michael after their father died. But still, does that stuff happen in real life? Well, unless you've been living under a rock these past couple of years, you know it does happen every day.

It doesn't matter what neighborhood you live in, from the suburbs to the ghetto, you can pick up any newspaper and read it for yourself. It even happened after the highlife of Eden, when Cain killed Abel. Not only in Genesis but throughout the Bible, there are countless stories of sibling rivalry that ended in beat downs, bloodshed, or even death.

Esau wanted to kill Jacob after the latter tricked him into trading his inheritance for some lentil soup (Genesis 25:29–34). Come to think of it, Esau was the dumb one! I wouldn't even trade one of my little Matchbox cars, let alone my birthright, for some lentil soup. Yuck! I know we Adventists love lentils, but not me. Now, if it was some chicken noodle soup from Panera Bread, the one with the bread bowl, that would have been tempting, that's the bomb! Or maybe even some beef stew; that's more like it! *Mmmmmm,* I'm getting hungry. (Focus, Willy, focus. This chapter is about family, Willy, not food. Ha!)

What about Joseph's brothers? They wanted to kill him after he told them about his dream that one day he'd be the *top dog* in charge. Not to mention they already hated *dude* after their father showed favoritism by making him a Gucci sweater. Them jokers beat him down, tore up his sweater, and threw him in a sewer. Then they went to McDonald's afterward! (Genesis 37:23–25). Now, that's some cold-blooded stuff. Even Jesus wasn't immune to family feud. His family thought He was *coo-coo for Cocoa Puffs*! (Mark 3:21).

But aren't family members supposed to love and protect each other? Sister Sledge had a song back in the day talking about "We are family!" But do we treat each other as such? I know some family members who haven't spoken for years, and when you ask them why, they can't remember! Why, if we're supposed to care for and look after each other, do we do the opposite?

At first it's all good. We love each other. We laugh together. Break bread together. We even share our dreams with our family members, etc. But let one of them jokers disagree with us and it's on like Donkey Kong! Then we hate, argue, fight, break away from, and share a few curse words with each other! Can I get a witness? And it's sad because it usually takes an event such as a parent's illness or death to bring that family close together again.

But why wait for something drastic like that to happen? Remember when Rodney King got beat up by those cops, and people started to loot and riot in Cali? Afterward, Rodney gave a speech where he asked, "Can't we all just get along?" Unfortunately, the answer to that is No! Yes, God wants us to. But we still haven't figured out the "getting along" part.

I remember when my wife and I were newly engaged, and counselors, friends, and family who were already married told us, "The first couple of years it's all a honeymoon." Shut up! No, it's *not*! My wife and I have had our share of fights, and we've been married for only two years. So much for the honeymoon! But it also can be great! And it is the same thing with family members. We have good times, but we also have our bad times.

Though I don't believe God designed it that way, I do believe that He allows it. He puts certain people together with different attitudes and styles so we can learn how to get along. Look at that motley crew of disciples He assembled! Stank fishermen strapped with swords, corrupt IRS agents, thieves, gangsters, and prostitutes! That sounds like the cast of a prison movie; instead, it was the roster of our early church.

You see, it ain't ever gonna be all good. Not while we are living here in this sinful, messed-up world.

That's why it's called the *pursuit* of happiness. Will Smith made an awesome movie by that name, and the term is also in our Constitution. It's a pursuit, a chase, something we strive for. Something we will never have in full as long as sin is still in the world.

Now, don't get me wrong, we will have it, but only in bits and pieces. Like going to Costco and getting some of them bomb samples they be giving out from their little concession stands. *Mmmmm.* Or like going to the food court at the mall, and the Chinese lady gives you a sample of the teriyaki chicken on a tooth-pick. One time my boy Casper and I went to the mall and a Chinese lady was like, "Nope. Not *you* again! None for you, no more!" She refused to serve me! I almost got karate kicked on the neck by a Jackie Chan–looking woman! Ha! Anyways, what I was trying to tell you before I got bombarded with food thoughts was that happiness comes only in bits and pieces, even for a Christian. And I think God allows it to give us a glimpse of the better life to come when we hit eternity.

Sometimes, God allows the heartbreaks and bad times for us to want to pursue something better. Imagine if it was all really good here. We probably wouldn't desire heaven so intensely. So, if this world isn't perfect, why do we think our *nappy-headed* cousin or your *smart-aleck* brother should be?

You know what the problem is? We are all *jacked up*! Yes, us! We all are; all of us. And deep inside we know it! But we don't want anybody else to know or to tell us we are. So before they discover what we are made of, we begin to find something wrong with them instead—especially if they are different from us!

We all have a *nutcase* in the family, someone who acts, thinks, or says stuff we would never say or do. Maybe they drink or smoke or even have a different religion from ours. Or maybe they are not believers at all. We can't stand them. Just because they're not like us! I guess it's a part of our sinful nature. You can even see it in little kids. Put a few kids in a room alone with only one toy, and you'll see the evil come out *with the quickness*!

Though we are all a part of God's great big family, like the song "We Are the World" says, we're still very much different from each other. And that's what we fail to see. If we could only get into our minds the fact that there's nothing wrong with being different! There isn't just one way of doing things.

But *nooooo*! We can't be wrong. God forbid. That family member (the nutcase) threatens the very way we live. We program ourselves to think they are the ones that are wrong because we are so perfect! (If that were truly the case, our mothers would have named us Jesus Jr.!) That might just be our insecurities. But instead of working out our differences, we attack them!

We get down and dirty and begin to call them names like "that heathen can't be a part of my family!" *Dude* must be adopted! His or her mother must've found them in a garbage can. We can't ever agree to disagree. We take the same approach with other denominations just because they worship on a different day than we do! Why do you think we have so many different religions? Maybe they wear jewelry or sing praise and worship music they hear on Christian radio and not from hymn books.

I have been treated horribly in some churches before, as though they were Cinderella's stepsisters or something! I once preached at a church for a whole week (from Sabbath to Sabbath), and the pastor didn't come even once to pray with or for me. I thought *dude* was on vacation, but like the youth director of the church told me, he just didn't like me. Just because you don't like the person, doesn't mean you can't still practice kindness. You don't have to be a jerk!

Years ago I went to New Mexico to preach. *Dude* that picked me up at the airport was from the other side of the train tracks. I'm from the hood, as you already know, but this dude looked like he was from Bel Air! I was tempted to ask him if he had a nephew named Fresh Prince. Anyway, right away, he looked like he had beef with me; he wouldn't even call me Willy. *Dude* called me William. Ha! He told me he didn't like me one bit. From the way I dressed to the way I spoke. Not even my number-one global smash hit sing-a-long, "Jesus Lovez Me" remix! What a *chump*! I should've hit the brakes on his car and let the air bag smack him upside his big head!

But then he floored me when he said the *but* word. Usually me and the word *but* don't get along, but *homie* said, "William, I do not like your style at all. I don't like how you dress; I don't like the way you talk. And I definitely don't like that 'Jesus loves me' rap thingy you do, BUT last year when you spoke at camp meeting, my daughter gave her life to Jesus and got baptized. In fact, you baptized her at the lake. So when the church board said that they didn't have any money to bring you in, my wife and I decided to pay all your expenses ourselves. You want to know why? Because the fact that we don't like your style doesn't mean you're wrong or that we are right. God obviously uses you. So I thank you, William Ramos."

Wow! I'm glad I didn't hit the brakes! Ha! You see? *Dude* gets it! Obviously, none of us were programmed the same way. We can be different and still try to get along. Amen.

It reminds me of the Fourth of July weekend like five years ago. I was at Hollywood beach with the family and something interesting happened. My nephews, who were five at the time (Jo-Jo, Big Lou, Li'l Pete, and Yahoo), were constantly fighting among themselves for any little reason. Suddenly, they were about to jump another little *dude* that was sitting with his family on the picnic table next to us.

Turns out that the little stranger was picking a fight with Yahoo, and his cousins came to the rescue. They surrounded little man and warned him, "Don't be messing with our cousin!" You see, even though they are always in some kind of dispute or nitpicking with each other, they know one thing: they're still family!

There's an old Arab saying that says something similar: "Me against my brother; my brother and me against my cousin; me, my brother, and my cousin against the stranger."

One time I was in a meeting with some pastors discussing a certain group from our own denomination who seem to always attack everything we did. They didn't like women wearing pants, married couples wearing wedding rings, drums in the church, etc. Some of us began to say very negative things about them like "Their mamas are so fat." (Nah, lemme stop. I probably was the only one thinking in my mind about the Yo

Mama jokes!) The negativity toward this group was there. So one of the pastors, my homie Manny Cruz, got up and said, "Yeah, they may be this and that . . . but at least they're ours."

"But at least they're ours." Wow! It kind of sounds like something John Gotti would say, doesn't it? I've always been fascinated with the Mafia, though I don't agree with anything they do, of course. Its members usually refer to each other as *La Cosa Nostra.* The English translation would be "our thing" or "this thing of ours." The word *ownership* comes to mind.

Speaking of which, in the opening scene of the movie *Gotti,* Armand Assante, who played the former mob boss, says, "Five or ten years from now, they gonna wish there was an American Cosa Nostra." In other words, he was saying, who's gonna take care of us like we do? Who else is going to love a son the way a mother does, even after finding out he's a drug addict? Who else is going to lend a cousin ten dollars when he knows he hasn't paid the twenty he borrowed last month? Who? Only family does that.

And, yeah, maybe in our family there are people who owe us money or brothers and sisters who haven't accepted God as Savior. And maybe there's a knuckle-head that just can't get it right or a black sheep or a pervert. But you know what? At least they're ours.

FREE Lessons at www.BibleStudies.com

It's easy to learn more about the Bible!

Call:
1-888-456-7933

Write:
Discover
P.O. Box 53055
Los Angeles, CA 90053